WORKER EMPOWERMENT IN A CHANGING ECONOMY

Jobs, Military Production, and the Environment

WORKER EMPOWERMENT IN A CHANGING ECONOMY

Jobs, Military Production, and the Environment

by Lucinda Wykle, Ward Morehouse, and David Dembo

Sponsored by the

NATIONAL TOXIC CAMPAIGN FUND/ LABOR INSTITUTE

Joint Project on Jobs And The Environment

THE APEX PRESS
New York

The Apex Press (formerly New Horizons Press) is an
imprint of the Council on International and Public Affairs, 777 United Nations Plaza, New York, New York
10017 (212/953-6920).

Library of Congress Cataloging-in-Publication Data:

Wykle, Lucinda.
    Worker empowerment in a changing economy : jobs, military
production, and the environment / by Lucinda Wykle, Ward
Morehouse, and David Dembo.
        p.   cm.
    ISBN 0-945257-33-3
    1. Manpower policy—United States. 2. Economic conversion
—United States. 3. Plant shutdowns—United States. 4. Environ-
mental policy—United States. I. Morehouse, Ward, 1929- .
II. Dembo, David. III. Title.
HD5724.W95 1991
331.11'0973—dc20   90-25834
                                                  CIP

Cover design by Janette Aiello
Typeset and printed in the United States of America

CONTENTS

FOREWORD

*by Anthony Mazzocchi, Secretary-Treasurer, Oil,
Chemical and Atomic Workers International Union*

The clash between our productive capacities and the tolerance of nature is heightening each day. Our prosperity is based on toxic substances and by-products that cause significant harm to our working people, their communities and the environment as a whole. If we continue to ignore this harm, as too many have done for too long, it will only come back to haunt us.

Our first and foremost task is to make workplaces that deal with toxic substances safe. There is much that can be done. Corporate America must be pressured to increase drastically its full-time maintenance staff to stop relying on unsafe outside contractors. Workers must be deputized in each facility to conduct day to day inspections under the protection of the law. Wherever possible we must find safer substitutes for harmful chemicals and processes. Profits should not come at the expense of the health, safety and environmental needs of our communities.

But in some cases, all of our best efforts may be insufficient to save our facilities and our jobs from destruction. In these instances a battle line is being drawn between jobs and the environment. This conflict is dividing our communities, pitting family against family, worker against environmentalist. And the conflict is growing ugly. The possibility of violence increases as those who are threatened with job loss rage against environmental activists.

All signs point to a heightening of this tension. Over the past decade millions of the better paying working class jobs have disappeared. Current economic woes suggest more and more will be destroyed in the 1990s. The workers I represent in the oil, chemical and atomic industry have their backs to the economic wall. Their frustration and anger is growing as they struggle to protect their livelihoods. In this economic context, when loggers and industrial workers lose their jobs, no decent paying alternatives will be found.

We all want to find a solution to this conflict. But first we must take a step closer to the every-day realities of work in a toxic facility. We must appreciate that these working people are literally on the front line of toxic exposure. They have watched their co-workers die in explosions. They know that their own life expectancies are far lower than the average citizen's. Yet they stay with their jobs. They stay there for the economic health of their families. They try to maintain a decent living standard by accepting many of these risks.

Many workers see the growing environmental clashes and they are angry and frustrated. They hold deep pro-environmentalist convictions. But none can advocate the elimination of his or her job. If they switched jobs they would have to cut their incomes in half, and probably lose all their benefits. Not many family people can afford to do that. They do not like being exposed on the job and they do not like what their facilities are doing to the environment. But they are not about to commit economic suicide.

Workers are also frustrated with the kind of well-intentioned proposals that others claim will provide them with new skill and new jobs. Retraining programs provide emergency relief to thousands of unemployed workers. But they do not solve the problem. Working people know that the only decent paying jobs in the new economy require advanced degrees. They also know that existing retraining programs *refuse* to support them if they want to go to college and have a real chance at decent employment. Instead, the existing programs are little more than subsidies to employers and training entrepreneurs who profit from workers' misfortune—and receive taxpayers' money for doing so.

At the same time, there is a deep well of hope and will among our members for any proposal based on a new vision of work and income. I have had the good fortune to travel around this country and promote a discussion of such a vision called a Superfund for Workers. This concept—which calls for full pay and benefits, and tuition for any workers losing their job for environmental reasons—has been positively received.

I have watched our older members who served in World War II and Korea recognize the roots of this proposal in the GI Bill of Rights. They remember that our society was capable of reconverting itself after the war and finding the funds to provide income and education for millions of returning soldiers. They know that when our country feels a transition is needed, something can be done.

Our younger workers with families see a different part of this vision. They see it as a way to escape from the toxic-filled world of traditional work. They are hungry for the chance to enter colleges and gain access to a new kind of work. They would jump at the chance to get paid to go to school.

They realize that such a program must be born out of a national movement. This kind of massive restructuring of our world of work cannot be won on a local or state basis. The nation as a whole must come to see it as a just solution.

I sincerely believe that we are ready for a new movement dedicated to redefining the relationship between work and income. We are also ready to advocate this concept for any worker who loses his or her job, or who has never had a job at all. We are tired of seeing so many of our brothers and sisters dumped on the economic wayside of America. Give us sabbaticals from the toxic world of work. Send us to school. Pay us our union wages, and for those of us without jobs, pay us the prevailing union wage and put welfare away. With full-income, the conflict between jobs and the environment will end.

Our vision entails a substantial pool of capital to fund this transition. Clearly, we are talking about tens of billions of dollars. But we know that the money is there. It is amazing how easily $500 billion is found to pay for the profligate practices of the savings and loan pirates. It is amazing how hundreds and billions of dollars are being set aside to clean up the waste at our military facilities. We certainly should be able to treat our working people as well as we treat dirt.

I am heartened to see a book that treats this concept with compassion and understanding. *Worker Empowerment in a Changing Economy* will help deepen the dialogue with all activists within the labor and the environmental communities. Its discussion of the GI Bill of Rights will help us remember what this country can do. Its discussion of the recent paltry attempts at job retraining will remind us that what we want is a new world of work at unionized wages, not short-term, narrow training that condemns us to a path of downward mobility.

The Superfund for Workers will be a tool of empowerment—

providing increasing control over their working lives. No longer will workers who have given their health and often their best working years to toxic-producing corporations have to settle for flipping hamburgers when their jobs are destroyed.

I also hope that this volume will help us see that the jobs versus environment question is fundamental to the progressive movement in our country. We need to be reminded again and again that this issue will not leave us alone. If we do not find a way to protect the hard-won livelihoods of workers in toxic industries, all of our progressive causes will be haunted. If we do not speak to the legitimate needs of these workers, self-appointed demagogues will rush into the vacuum and tear us apart.

PREFACE

The purpose of this book is to provoke debate on the future of American workers in a period of rapid and pervasive industrial restructuring. We believe that such restructuring is inescapable in the 1990s and beyond as we confront the consequences of the end of the Cold War and decades of abuse of our environment.

In the decade just beginning, the lives of millions of working people in the United States will be profoundly affected by this industrial restructuring. The Superfund for Workers, articulated and advocated in the pages following, constitutes a response to this restructuring that we are convinced will be both empowering to workers and beneficial to society. The very act of debating this concept will compel attention to the welfare of American working men and women and their families— a condition all too often ignored in past periods of turbulence and rapid change.

While solidly rooted in twentieth century public policy through the GI Bill, the Superfund for Workers represents a fundamental shift or extension in public policy in at least three vital ways:

1. It recognizes education as work where it serves an important social purpose.
2. It provides an opportunity for displaced workers from environmentally polluting and military production industries to prepare themselves for entirely different careers.
3. As such, it also provides these workers with real choices in shaping the balance of their working lives.

All this makes the Superfund for Workers a tool of empowerment for working people. But it also represents a means of nurturing what many thoughtful observers believe is our greatest national asset in a rapidly changing post-industrial world—namely, our "human capital," the working men and women of these United States.

The Superfund for Workers is thus informed by a vision of a more just social order and a more vigorous economic democracy. It is also informed by a vision of an environmentally sustainable, non-militarized economy—a vision yet to be achieved as we enter the last decade of the twentieth century.

While the Superfund for Workers has important economic implications, it must be understood that in the final analysis the issue is political. The struggle to realize this tool of worker empowerment will challenge existing patterns of concentration of economic and political power in late twentieth century America. That struggle will be successful only if all those who are committed to building a more just, sustainable, and democratic future join hands.

We acknowledge with thanks the assistance of friends and fellow workers in producing this book: John O'Connell for research assistance; Peggy Hurley for typesetting; Cynthia T. Morehouse and Margot Bettauer for copy editing and proof reading; and Tony Mazzocchi for the Foreword. It is only appropriate that he should write the Foreword to this book since he is truly the father of the concept of a Superfund for Workers. Many others contributed through argument and debate on underlying issues and critical feedback on successive drafts of the manuscript, including Les Leopold and Mike Merrill of the Labor Institute; Sanford Lewis and Gary Cohen of the National Toxic Campaign Fund; Richard Grossman, the editor of the *Monkey Wrenching Gazette;* and Richard Miller of the Oil, Chemical and Atomic Workers International Union, in which we are proud to be rank-and-file members.

The Labor Institute and the National Toxic Campaign Fund have initiated a joint project on Labor and the Environment. We would like to acknowledge gratefully their co-sponsorship of this book. The fact that labor and environmental groups are working together to advance the Superfund for Workers is an indication that it is time for such a program to be seriously considered.

Needless to say, none of the foregoing should be held reponsible for what follows. That responsibility is ours alone.

INTRODUCTION

America's Mess

- Damage to the environment surrounding atomic weapons plants run for the U.S. government by major corporations such as Union Carbide, Dupont, and General Electric is finally being acknowledged by the Department of Energy. The latest estimate by DOE to clean up such sites is $91.7 billion over the next 20 years.

- Calculations of the dangers posed to health and safety and the environment from existing industrial hazardous waste sites were revised in 1985 when it was estimated that a minimum of 10,000 such sites needed to be addressed and would require 50 years and at least $100 billion dollars to contain or clean up.

- The passage of the Clean Air Act in 1990 makes it abundantly clear that corporations and governments—both local and national—are unwilling to meet requirements of the original Clean Air Act. The newer, admittedly inadequate and long overdue, version acknowledges the abuses of the environment by industrial pollution, although it does little to correct them.

- Current debate over the prospect of Global Warming and the need for drastic measures to counteract potential dire consequences likewise acknowledges the devastation of our atmosphere by industrial processes and products, the unrestrained use of private transportation, and wasteful energy policies.

We can expect continued revelations of the massive destruction of our environment to benefit this country's industrial and military elite. There are hundreds of hazardous waste sites not yet on the Superfund list to be cleaned up; U.S. industry continues to generate as much as 400 billion pounds of toxic chemicals each year; some 4.5 billion pounds of toxics are emitted into the air each year; and we have not even begun to dispose of the huge amounts of deadly waste from nuclear power plants and atomic weapons production. The cumulative magnitude of these efforts (not near a complete listing of what is urgently needed) is quite enough to indicate the huge task confronting our society.

Obstacles to a Sustainable Future

Cleaning up the environment, reducing use of toxics, and converting to a peacetime economy all involve extensive industrial restructuring in response to fundamental shifts in society's priorities. These in turn are reflected in far-reaching changes in public policy. After 40 years of industrial growth in post-war America, during which we have mounted a massive assault on the biosphere, the American people are beginning to understand that we must make far-reaching changes in what we produce and how we produce it if we are to preserve that biosphere for future generations.

This means drastic reductions in the use of toxic chemicals; there is no other way. In poll after poll, Americans in overwhelming percentages have said that we must clean up the environment even if it costs more money.

Similarly, there has been a fundamental shift in public attitudes toward national security policy with the end of the Cold War. Even the current aggression in the Middle East does not alter that fundamental shift in our priorities. Rather, such intervention introduces another imperative for industrial restructuring—namely, the vital need to build a more energy efficient economy less dependent on a single energy source.

These imperatives for public policy are all interrelated. There is substantial correlation between defense production and those industries which are early targets in any comprehensive attack on environmental pollution. The same can be said of energy-intensive modes of production whether in industry or agriculture: they tend to be more damaging to the environment than energy-efficient or conserving methods.

If, in the process of industrial restructuring toward a cleaner, healthier, and sustainable future, decisions concerning the distribution of costs of such restructuring remain in the hands of government and industry alone, workers and the middle class will continue to bear the heaviest burden in reducing the use of toxics and cutting wasteful military expenditures. We need a more democratic way to address disruptions caused by industrial restructuring for a cleaner environment and less militarized economy—a way by which those whose lives will be most directly affected are empowered to make meaningful choices about their own futures.

Otherwise, corporations will continue to use the same tactics which have proved to be so successful in the past to resist substantive change, and government will continue to support them. One of the most widespread of these tactics used by industry to avert new regulatory policies is to argue that plants will close and jobs will be lost as a result. When industry uses such tactics, they are engaging in job blackmail.[1]

Job blackmail is a major obstacle to the industrial restructuring essential for a cleaner, more peaceful America of the twenty-first century. It is a strategy widely used by company managements to resist change and to divide workers and local communities.The technique is disarmingly simple. Tell workers they will lose their jobs if changes not wanted by management are introduced:

- Introduce more stringent environmental regulations and we will have to close the plant because we will no longer be competitive.

- Your jobs will go to some low-wage pollution haven in the Third World where government is more "reasonable" about such matters.

- Cut off the next Pentagon contract and we will simply shut down, laying off all of you production workers.

The litany is essentially the same. Job blackmail is a powerful and manipulative tool used by management fighting change. It pits workers against the surrounding community, defying their common interest in a cleaner, healthier environment. It becomes the tactical basis for all manner of "give-backs" in collective bargaining with unions, thus running the gamut of labor relations. The objective of this book is to present a strategy for overcoming job blackmail as a major obstacle to cleaning up the environment and shifting to a more energy-efficient peacetime economy.

We propose a straightforward solution to job blackmail: a Superfund for workers displaced by the industrial restructuring vital to environmental cleanup and conversion to a more energy-efficient demilitarized economy. The Superfund as outlined in Chapter V would provide an opportunity for such workers to prepare themselves for fundamentally different careers and to make the transition to those careers. It rests on five basic assumptions. The first is that being serious about environmental cleanup—and the attendant tasks of converting to a more energy efficient demilitarized economy—will involve far-reaching changes in the U.S. economy affecting millions of workers. Any dynamic economy is, of course, changing all the time. But over the next decade and beyond, much more far-reaching change than what might be labeled "business as usual" will be occurring. We have identified in the next chapter some of the industrial sectors that will have to be affected if we really are going to clean up the environment.

The second assumption is that, with this restructuring, there will be far fewer industrial production jobs paying decent wages. The post-war trend, greatly accelerated in the 1980s, has seen higher-paying jobs in the goods-producing sector of the U.S. economy decline precipitously as a percentage of the total work force (from 36.1 percent in the 1960s and 30.9 percent in the 1970s to 25.7 percent in the 1980s). Low-wage jobs in the service sector have grown dramatically. The result is that the average real wage of industrial workers in the United States is now lower than it has been in any year since 1961. We present an analysis of these trends in Chapter III.

The third assumption is that most people do not actually enjoy working in industrial jobs. Many industrial production jobs that pay decent wages are monotonous and hazardous. The long-term health effects on such workers are increasingly recognized. We believe many workers, given a reasonable choice—i.e., a healthier, safer job at roughly comparable pay—would choose work which did not involve undermining their health and running the risk of serious accident.

A fourth vital assumption concerns the need to build greater equity in the work place. Women and minorities face far greater difficulties in finding decent jobs at a fair wage. The Superfund for Workers will provide a mechanism for enabling such persons to make a basic shift into new careers with better working conditions and perhaps better pay.

The Superfund for Workers also comes to grips with another inequity in the work place between those who bear and those who are shielded from the burdens of industrial restructuring. Companies already have some protection against changes brought about by more rigorous environmental standards—e.g., the Federal Insecticide, Fungicide, and Rodenticide Act, which provides government compensation for lost sales and for the cost of storing a product banned or severely restricted under the act. Senior corporate officials protect themselves from industrial restructuring with golden parachutes, sometimes truly offensive in the largess they bestow. But workers rarely have any such protection when they are displaced. The Superfund for Workers would go a long way in addressing this kind of inequity as well.

Finally, the Superfund rests on the assumption that "human capital" is our most vital national resource and must be not only sustained but nurtured. The Superfund for Workers is precisely that—a means of sustaining and nurturing that most valuable national resource. It is a response to what has been called the new "era of human capital."[2] In a very real sense, it can be seen as an instrument for reversing the trends of recent decades in "deskilling" workers and instead accelerating the process of "reskilling" society.

These various assumptions are examined in greater detail in subsequent chapters in this book which also explore, especially in Chapter IV, the precedents in public policy for the Superfund for Workers. While the concept may seem revolutionary to some, it is in fact simply a logical evolution of past initiatives designed to help large groups of affected Americans adapt to a changing work environment. By far the most notable precedent is the GI Bill of Rights—a tool of empowerment which enabled millions of Americans to shift from military service to civilian work through the medium of higher education and to shape their future lives through their own choices.

Some of the difficulties encountered in implementing these past initiatives provide the basis for anticipating problems in designing and instituting the Superfund for Workers. These questions are discussed in Chapter VI. The final chapter in the book addresses the crucial issue of making it happen—i.e., the politics of creating a Superfund for Workers. We see the 1990s as a decade characterized by the emergence of several reinforcing trends. These include a populist reaction against the sharp increase in disparities between the rich and the poor of the 1980s, the emergence of a political movement of working people, the accelerating impact of environmental cleanup on and conversion to a peacetime economy, and an increasing awareness of the unfair practices of the past. All of these, we believe, can generate the political will necessary to make ideas like the Superfund for Workers happen.

All those committed to cleaning up the environment, reducing the use of toxics, and demilitarizing the economy—whether workers or community groups, environmentalists or peace activists—must work together in demanding the creation of a Superfund for Workers. The strident cries of the rich and powerful can be heard already: "We can't afford it!"

In the last decade, we spent over $2.3 trillion on the biggest corporate welfare program in the history of the world—the Pentagon budget. And we are now embarked on another welfare program for the rich in the $500 billion bailout of savings and loan associations. Of course we can afford the Superfund. The issue is political, not economic.

The struggle will be long and hard—all the more reason we must start now to inform and mobilize at the grass roots. The Superfund for Workers is an absolutely vital tool for community groups that are fighting industry and government to stop polluting. With it, they will no longer be in conflict with workers, but instead work together in building a new and more democratic economy safe for all living things.

NOTES

1. The concept of job blackmail as related to environment and labor has been discussed most thoroughly in Richard Kazis and Richard Grossman, *Fear at Work: Job Blackmail, Labor and the Environment,* New York: Pilgrim Press, 1982. A revised edition will shortly be published by New Society Publishers.

2. Robert Reich of the Harvard Business School suggests that "our standard of living depends increasingly on returns to intellectual capital, rather than to physical or financial capital." ("Members Only," *The New Republic,* June 26, 1989, p. 16.)

II.

THE ENVIRONMENTAL CRISIS, MILITARY PRODUCTION, AND DISPLACED WORKERS

Job Loss/Job Blackmail

For three decades environmental degradation has assumed growing importance at all levels of our society. At the grass roots, citizens are fighting the siting of hazardous facilities and dumps and protesting the use and production of harmful products. Local and state governments are compelled to deal with hazardous waste, land use, and air and water pollution problems. At the Federal level, companies, state and local governments, national environmental organizations, regulatory agencies, such as the EPA and others, attempt to assert their own interests in cleaning up or avoiding or delaying the cleanup of the environment.

In some cases, these efforts have affected facilities in localized areas. For example, a hazardous gas-producing plant is closed down or a waste site is closed or moved. In other cases, national or state-wide legislation might affect entire industries or communities across the country, as with efforts to protect the ozone layer and clean air, clean water, and hazardous waste legislation.

Efforts to clean up the environment and reduce or curtail (especially nuclear) weapons production inevitably are confronted by two issues used by those who oppose such efforts: the possible negative impact on profits and the possible negative impact on jobs. Statements regarding the impacts such efforts might have on jobs are very often used by industry to mask the real reason for their opposition: a possible impact on the bottom line.

In fact, the threat of job loss has assumed great importance in everything from environmental, worker, and public health and safety legislation to international trade issues and possible cuts in the Pentagon budget. Industry has been very successful in using the jobs issue at all levels. At local levels, when a community threatens to shut down a plant due to health, safety, and environmental concerns, a company can cite possible job losses to workers in the plant and to local government to great effect. The UNOCAL/Taos, New Mexico; the Champion/Canton, North Carolina; and the Ashland Oil cases discussed below are examples.

On an industry-wide basis, job loss arguments are an effective way of derailing environmental activism. The battles over saving the Tongass National Forests in Alaska and the Redwood stands in Northern California have been countered by arguments of the timber industry that thousands of lumberjack and lumber-processing jobs would be lost. At the national level, efforts at strengthening the Clean Air and Clean Water Acts, reducing the Pentagon budget, enforcing the Occupational Safety and Health Act (OSHA), the Toxic Substances Control Act (TOSCA), the Resource Conservation and Recovery Act (RCRA), and other regulations have been met by similar arguments.

Any direct negative relationship between environmental regulations and profits and jobs of companies engaged in the production and use of toxics is certainly not borne out by data on the industry as a whole. Since the passage of the original Clean Air Act Amendments in 1970, at least 18 major laws regulating the environment have been passed. They are listed in Table 1. During that time, the employment record of companies in the chemical and pharmaceutical industry has indeed fluctuated. As Figure 1 shows, employment was around 600,000 in the 1970s, reaching a height of 633,000 in 1979—long after many of the major environmental regulations had gone into effect. The subsequent

Table 1
FEDERAL LAWS RELATED TO THE ENVIRONMENT

Regulating the Environment   **Date Enacted**

Clean Air Act Amendments of 1970	1970
Resource Recovery Act — amends the Solid Waste Disposal Act	1970
Water Pollution Control Act Amendments	1972
Ocean Dumping Act — a title of the Marine Protection Research and Sanctuaries Act	1972

Regulating Toxic Substances

Federal Insecticide, Fungicide and Rodenticide Act — amends the Federal Environmental Pesticide Control Act	1972
Safe Drinking Water Act — amends the Public Health Service Act	1974
Resource Conservation and Recovery Act (RCRA) — amends the Resource Recovery Act, which focuses on hazardous wastes	1976
Toxic Substances Control Act	1976
Clean Air Act Amendments of 1977	1977
Clean Water Act of 1977 — amends the Water Pollution Control Act	1977
Federal Insecticide, Fungicide and Rodenticide Act Amendments of 1978	1978
Comprehensive Environmental Response, Compensation, and Liability Act (Superfund)	1980
Hazardous and Solid Waste Amendments — amend the Resource Conservation and Recovery Act	1984
Superfund Amendments and Reauthorization Act (SARA)	1986

Regulating Consumer and Worker Health & Safety

Federal Railroad Safety Act — regulates shipment of hazardous substances by railroad	1970
Occupational Safety and Health Act (OSHA) — regulates workplace safety & health	1970
Consumer Product Safety Act	1972
Hazardous Materials Transportation Act — regulates the transport of toxic substances	1975
Federal Mine Safety and Health Act (MSHA) — regulates mine safety & health 1977	1977

Source: Adapted from: Conservation Foundation, "State of the Environment: An Assessment at Mid-Decade" (Washington, DC: 1984) as cited in OCAW/Labor Institute, *Hazardous Waste Workbook,* New York: New Horizons Press, 1990, p. 14.

Figure 1
PRODUCTION OR NONSUPERVISORY EMPLOYMENT IN THE CHEMICAL AND PHARMACEUTICAL INDUSTRIES, 1970-1989

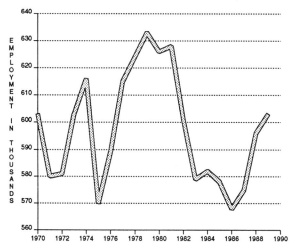

PROFITS IN THE CHEMICAL AND PHARMACEUTICAL INDUSTRIES, 1970-1989

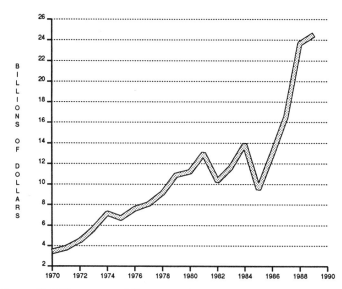

Source: U.S. Department of Commerce, Bureau of Economic Analysis, *Survey of Current Business,* September issues, 1971, 1973, 1975, 1977, 1979, 1981, 1983, 1985, 1987, 1989, and 1990.

decline appears to have followed the economic slump and recovery far more than any changes in environmental laws and regulations.

It is clearly evident from Figure 1 that there is no direct relationship between the ability of companies in the chemical and pharmaceutical industry to make a profit and the laying off of workers. For example, from 1979 to 1980, profits increased 3.0 percent but 7,000 jobs were cut. From 1982 to 1983, profits rose 12.8 percent but 22,000 jobs were cut, and from 1985 to 1986, profits rose 35.2 percent but 10,000 workers lost their jobs.[1]

One basic argument against job blackmail is based on equity: Workers, who in many cases have had their health impaired through employment in toxic industries, should not bear the brunt of efforts to clean up the environment. But there are other arguments as well. Workers are our first line of defense against hazardous operating conditions and abuses by poorly regulated industrial plants and military contractors. They are among the most knowledgeable when it comes to possibilities for operating hazardous facilities more safely and for cleaner production through reductions in the use of toxics. And certainly American workers benefit society in many other ways, from paying taxes to purchasing goods and services.

Thus, threats to our jobs from plant closings or transfers overseas are of immediate concern to all of us. And these threats are used as a wedge to divide workers from communities. The following examples are meant to demonstrate the ways in which potential job loss is used by different sides in the debate over environmental cleanup, toxic use reduction and reducing military production. They raise a number of questions regarding the use of "job loss" as a weapon:

- Is the projected job loss real or illusory?

- Is the degree of job loss intentionally exaggerated or minimized?

- Are the jobs lost replaced by new jobs?

- Are those new jobs going to the people who lost jobs?

- Are these new jobs qualitatively the same or better than the old ones?

- Is the job loss argument used to mask other, less politically motivating concerns (e.g. profit impact)?

- If job loss is to come through attrition, what happens to a community which was dependent on those incomes?

One point from the examples is clear, however, the job loss argument is a powerful one. It places workers in the position of having to fight for their economic survival and often drives a wedge between groups that would otherwise join efforts to better their health and environment. And it is an argument which can only be undermined to the benefit of workers and their communities by providing those workers with real alternatives to their current means of support.

Examples of Job Blackmail

In a pioneering work on the subject, Richard Grossman and Richard Kazis provide several examples of job blackmail as it has been used to counter threats posed to profits from unionization, regulation, and other actions to strengthen the political and economic power of employees and community members, and to improve health and safety of workers and the environment.[2] Since the battles over the original Clean Air Act legislation began more than two decades ago, job blackmail has been used increasingly to argue against environmental legislation and actions.

In 1971, for example, when Union Carbide was ordered by the U.S. Environmental Protection Agency (EPA) to comply with clean air standards at its Marietta, Ohio plant, the company claimed that it would have to shut two boilers and lay off over 600 workers in order to comply with the law. When the Oil, Chemical and Atomic Workers International Union and local citizens supported the EPA efforts, Carbide backed down, met the pollution control deadline, and laid off no workers.[3]

More recent battles over saving our national forests have been reduced to arguments on the part of the lumber industry and government agencies heavily influenced by the industry that significant numbers of jobs are threatened by any efforts to halt clearcutting of forests.[4] For example, the U.S. Forest Service claims that saving the old growth forests and the spotted owl in Northern California would cost 28,000 jobs.

Environmentalists point out that those jobs are jeopardized by the industry efforts to export raw lumber to Japan. According to one estimate, such exports result in a loss of between four and five jobs for every million board feet of unprocessed logs exported. The Oregon Natural Resources Council estimated that some 4,800 mill jobs and

2,700 related jobs were "lost" because of the exports of raw logs in one year (1988) in that state alone.[5]

Proponents of a statewide initiative in California to ban clearcutting—Forests Forever—claim that 40,000 timber jobs could be regained by curtailing exports of unprocessed trees.[6]

Additional job loss comes from efforts by the logging industry to cut down the forests before any legislation is passed—in effect, destroying any future there might have been in sustainable management of the resources.

Likewise, estimates of the number of jobs which may be lost due to efforts at preserving the Tongass National Forest in Alaska are put at 1,500. In that case, the U.S. Forest Service subsidizes logging (including Japanese-owned mills) at a cost of $40 million a year in exchange for a promise of job creation—$40 million a year for 1,500 jobs. As the *New York Times* editorialized, "it would be cheaper just to pay each logger $36,000 a year—and it would protect the environment besides."[7]

Community residents concerned about the environment in Taos, New Mexico, are engaged in a battle with a subsidiary of UNOCAL (the 47th largest U.S. industrial corporation with 1988 profits of $480 million). UNOCAL mines molybdenum there and argues that "shutting down the mine would severely disrupt the lives of a lot of people." But in the last five years, due to the falling price of molybdenum, the mine has cut employment by two-thirds and the unemployment rate is now over 15 percent. Only 300 workers are left at the mine.[8]

Ironically, these cutbacks make the corporation's job loss arguments against environmentalists all the more effective. The lack of alternate job opportunities in the area means those now laid off have little prospect of finding jobs at comparable wages locally, or, as we discuss in Chapter III, anywhere in the U.S.

A similar employment situation confronts workers and community residents in North Carolina. The Champion International paper mill has been operating in Western North Carolina for over eighty years. The mill is located in Canton on the Pigeon River which flows from North Carolina into Tennessee. Champion is one of the largest employers in the western part of the state, providing 2,000 jobs which pay up to $40,000 a year plus benefits, making the average annual income in Haywood County $12,500 compared to $6,800 in Cocke County, Tennessee downriver from the plant.[9]

Though the paper mill has brought economic benefits to the region, it has also brought environmental destruction and hazards to the health of communities along the river. One town with about 780 residents in

Cocke county had an estimated 167 people with cancer according to an informal survey, and high levels of dioxin and other toxins have been found in the water.[10]

In 1985, in response to protests from some community residents, the federal Environmental Protection Agency blocked renewal of the mill's waste-water-discharge permit, and ordered the company to clean up the river. The order set off a debate that still divides affected communities. Champion claimed it would be forced to shut down the plant to comply with Tennessee standards for its effluent.[11]

The media appears to have fueled the conflict with forecasts of economic depression based on Champion's claims that it would be forced to close its doors or lay off large numbers of workers, and framed the argument in the context of choosing between jobs or a cleaner river.

In 1989, Champion said they could comply with the EPA standard by cutting 1,000 jobs. The EPA said there was no concrete evidence that the loss of jobs would be a result of meeting the standard. In fact, the EPA stated that Champion had indicated that regardless of the outcome of the permit, they would decrease the number of workers at the mill in order to modernize and improve the plant's profitability.[12] But as one 51-year-old worker asked, "What do you do when you're my age and faced with the prospect of being thrown out on the street? What am I gonna do, get a job at McDonald's?"[13]

The issue has pitted Western North Carolinians against Tennessee residents, neighbor against neighbor, and workers against communities and environmentalists. The reaction of the Governors of the two states was symbolic. The Governor of Tennessee canoed the Pigeon River, declaring it a "sewer," while North Carolina Governor Jim Martin said the issue came down to "2,000 jobs vs. the color of a river."[14]

In 1990 the issue remains unresolved, though tempers have cooled somewhat, as the immediate threat to jobs has lessened. The company's job loss estimates in December 1989 stood at 1,000 over a three-year period. In June, 1990 Champion eliminated 300 positions in the process of modernizing the plant, though the company said these jobs represented retirements and transfers and would not affect workers now at the plant. In addition, 1,000 non-union construction jobs were provided by modernization efforts at the plant.[15] It is not clear whether these modernization efforts would have been undertaken regardless of EPA's stand on issuing the permit, or how many jobs may or may not be lost due to the water standard. Nor is it clear what the effect of 300 fewer jobs at the plant will be on the community.

What is clear, however, is that the threat of job loss was effective.

Champion and EPA reached an agreement that the company must meet Tennessee's standard over a three-year period, but rather than meet it at the site of the plant in Canton, it would be tested 25 miles downriver at the Tennessee/North Carolina border which would give the effluent a chance to dilute.

Ashland Oil in Kentucky provides yet another example of the importance of the jobs issue, especially when the company in question is a major employer in the area. Ashland Oil company is the largest corporation in Kentucky. It provides 1,700 jobs at its Catlettsburg plant alone. Catlettsburg is located at the junction of three states: Ohio, West Virginia, and Kentucky.

Ashland Oil's environmental and safety record is far from spotless. The company has been cited for hundreds of pollution and safety violations over the last decade. The company paid out $310,000 in air pollution fines from 1985 to 1986, and has attempted to use equipment malfunctions as an excuse for excess emissions (86 times in 1989) to avoid additional fines. In 1988, the company spilled 500,000 gallons of diesel fuel into the Monongahela River.[16]

Several residents in the Tri-state region resorted to lawsuits in the mid-to-late 1980s against Ashland to force it to reduce its emissions. Four people were awarded a $10.3 million verdict in 1990 against Ashland, and the company is facing hundreds of other lawsuits totaling approximately $3 billion. The lawsuits and activism against Ashland have deeply divided local communities. Employees of Ashland have lined up against community groups concerned about health and environmental issues.

Even though the company has not made specific threats that it will shut down or lay off workers if the lawsuits continue, the fear of that possibility is evident. As local residents indicated in letters-to-the-editor of local papers, the "jobs versus the environment" argument has been effectively introduced:

> . . . Ashland Oil's management has been successful at convincing its workers and friends that it can't run a refinery without using the surroundings as a dumping grounds. Jobs or health, you can't have both—or so AOI wants us to believe. What if Ashland Oil worked as hard at controlling the plant as it does at trying to control public opinion? . . . Then, maybe it wouldn't have to ask us to choose between jobs and health."[17]

> My solution to the problem was to spend $1 at the local car wash and spray away the "fallout." I am not condoning pol-

lution and I am concerned with the health and well-being of
my family, but . . . Ashland Oil is a vital part of this community. We need the jobs that it provides. What will we do
if it becomes unprofitable for it to do business in this area?[18]

The manner in which such concerns are manifested on a national
level are evident in a number of recent legislative compromises. The
1990 farm bill, for example, does not include a provision sought by environmentalists which would have barred the export of pesticides
banned in the United States. A similar executive order existed under the
Carter administration, but Reagan was quick to overturn it. The Bush
administration and the EPA and Department of Agriculture took
industry's side, agreeing that too many jobs would be lost as a result.[19]

The recent battle over amendments to the Clean Air Act provides
another example. As Congress attempted to compromise over legislation to combat acid rain, global warming, and ozone depletion, an industry-sponsored study on the risks to jobs of such initiatives was made
public by the CONSAD Research Corporation of Pittsburgh.

The CONSAD study concludes that there is "*no doubt* that, across
the CAA Amendment titles studied [air toxics jobs impacts, acid deposi-
tion control/energy-intensive industry impacts, and permitting and
small business impacts], there are a minimum of several hundred
thousands of jobs at various levels of severity of risk . . ." and that ". . .
this study leaves little doubt that a *minimum* of two hundred thousand
(plus) jobs will be quickly lost . . ."[20]

But the study does leave a lot of doubt. First, by ignoring job gains
from pollution control technology and any other benefits of decreased
emissions. Second, by focusing on community job loss rather than net
job loss. Thus, if a plant is moved or production shifted from a plant in
one area to another, even if the total number of jobs remains the same,
the study counts the shift in jobs from one area to another as jobs lost.
And third, by emphasizing the worst case scenario in its summary,
despite the fact that the study itself concludes that the provisions could
result in job *losses* of only 19,000. The study's two million figure is for
"jobs adversely affected," not jobs lost.

Such findings are then used to bolster industry's claims against any
legislation which might affect their bottom line. A recent advertisement
in the *New Republic* did just that. The ad reproduced on the next page,
was sponsored by an industry group calling itself the Clean Air Working Group. It bases its opposition to the Clean Air Act Amendments as
passed by the Senate on the possible loss of 750,000 jobs.[21] Even the
Wall Street Journal acknowledges this political manipulation of the data

Burning Your Money Won't Clean the Air.

Cleaner air is a national priority for everyone. So is maintaining a strong economy.

We don't have to choose between them. We can have both.

But not if Congress thinks Americans have money to burn.

The U.S. Senate just passed an unnecessarily expensive piece of clean air legislation that could cost up to $50 billion annually. The House is working on a similar measure that, while less expensive, imposes severe restrictions that also could limit economic growth in various regions of the country.

These bills will hit American workers and consumers hard. The Senate version could eliminate up to 750,000 jobs and seriously impact 3 million others. Prices will increase – for electricity, fuel, and many other essential goods and services. Don't let the House of Representatives add even more unreasonable requirements to burden consumers and businesses that are the backbone of a strong economy.

Everyone wants cleaner air. And everyone wants Congress to pass new clean air legislation this year. But, Americans deserve a clean air law they can afford. Let your Representatives in Congress know that burning up our prosperity won't clear the skies.

CAWG CLEAN AIR WORKING GROUP

Let's protect our environment *and* our economy.

Clean Air Working Group, 818 Connecticut Ave., N.W., Washington, D.C. 20006, 202/857-0370

Source: Clean Air Working Group advertisement, *The New Republic,* May 14, 1990, p. 23.

in an article entitled "Air Bill's Cost-Benefit Data Look Very Foggy Up Close."[22]

This is not a recent tactic. In 1978, Gould, Inc. ran a full-page ad in the *Wall Street Journal* showing the Statue of Liberty with a noose around her neck. The ad stated in part: "As the noose of overregulation tightens, it threatens to strangle creativity and invention—and therefore, productivity and increased employment . . ."[23]

It is irresponsible to say that all workers in industries affected by environmental legislation will be in danger of losing their jobs. As long as environmental cleanup remains a tug-of-war between various politicized factions, the number of workers affected will remain well below the maximum mentioned in the types of industry-sponsored research discussed above. Industry has exaggerated possible losses in the past, and as the last 20 years have shown, industry is very adept at eluding or minimizing the impact of such regulations.[24]

But studies sponsored by industry are not the only ones that are misleading on the question of jobs. The need for a Superfund for Workers is evident in a study reported in *Ambio* last year. Using data from 1985, the authors attempt to show that measures implemented to control pollution and meet regulations designed to lessen air, water, and solid waste pollution have actually resulted in increased employment to the tune of some 167,000 jobs.[25] In 1988, the same consulting firm said that as many as 2,963,400 jobs were created by the pollution abatement and control industry.[26]

What these authors include in data in one table in the *Ambio* article (see Table 2) but fail to mention in the text, is that 23 percent of identified job gains from business investment in pollution abatement and control were secretarial positions, 10.1 percent were bookkeepers, 4.2 percent were shipping and receiving clerks, and 5.9 percent were janitors. Thus, of 28,863 jobs identified by occupation as being created in 1985 from pollution abatement and control, 43.6 percent were for jobs in what are typically lower-paying occupations. Many of the remainder are in areas requiring specialized skills, such as computer systems analysts, surveyors, and electrical and electronics engineers.[27] It is unlikely that these "new" jobs will be filled by production workers who have lost jobs due to environmental cleanup.

That environmental regulation is not actually the reason for most plant closings is evident in a recent analysis of permanent plant closings. The Oil, Chemical and Atomic Workers International Union looked at the actual reasons for plant closings and layoffs in the United States from January 1980 through May 1986. Of the 224 closings listed,

Table 2

JOBS CREATED BY 1985 INVESTMENT IN POLLUTION ABATEMENT AND CONTROL

Occupation	Jobs Created
Computer Systems Analysts	393
Chemical Engineers	489
Electrical and Electronics Engineers	1,022
Geologists	356
Operations Research and Systems Analysts	504
Health Technologists and Technicians	169
Surveyors	185
Purchasers, Wholesale and Retail	154
Construction Inspectors	142
Manufacturing Industries Sales Reps	966
Bookkeepers	2,904
Secretaries	6,761
Shipping and Receiving Clerks	1,219
Excavating, Grading and Road Machine Operators	787
Machinists	2,193
Heavy Equipment Mechanics	3,775
Metal Molders	303
Plumbers	1,278
Structural Metal Craftsmen	204
Assemblers	2,811
Janitors	1,705
Other	543
Total	**28,863**

Source: Adapted from Roger Bezdek et al, "The Economic and Employment
  Effects of Investments in Pollution Abatement and Control Technologies,"
  Ambio, Volume XVIII, No. 5, 1989, p. 278.

only 12 gave environmental considerations or regulations as a reason
for closing. Most of the closings were actually in response to economic
conditions or obsolete plants and equipment.[28]

Job Loss through Reduction in Military Production

Job loss in industries affected by environmental protection is not the only area of economic adjustment creating need for a Superfund for Workers. Job loss through cutbacks in defense spending is another. It is also an area in which projections of job loss play a major political role in arguing for or against moves toward a less militarized economy. To the extent that the Pentagon is able to move troops in massive numbers around the world to protect the profits of Exxon, Mobil, and others, job loss will certainly be minimal. But projections prior to this latest display of military aggression show that any real effort to reduce Pentagon spending might result in substantial job loss.

According to an article in the *National Journal,* between 1986 and 1989, 140,000 defense industry jobs were lost—prior to reductions in the military budget.[29] A recent study (prior to the latest buildup) by DRI/McGraw-Hill predicted that 600,000 jobs will be lost by 1994. That study, reported by the *Christian Science Monitor,* estimates that some 10 to 20 percent of those workers will not have skills easily transferable to civilian uses.[30]

But efforts at conversion of facilities from military to civilian production, if they are successful, will have a mitigating influence on job loss. Several studies in the last few years show that there is often net new job creation both from efforts at pollution control, including toxic use reduction, and in conversion of military facilities to civilian use.

The Center for Public Interest Research has just completed a study of toxic use reduction and resulting job loss. Through both case studies and a review of the literature, it appears that jobs may actually be created through reductions in an industrial plant's use of toxics if, for example, it then creates a market for other companies to use its cleaner process.[31]

The Department of Defense, similarly, has found in a study of the conversions of military bases to civilian use in the last 25 years, that there has been a net increase in employment at those facilities of civilian workers—138,138 new jobs compared with 93,424 Department of Defense civilian jobs lost at 100 former bases.[32]

But neither of these studies tells the full story. In the case of the Defense Department study, there is no attempt to determine how many of the former workers were able to obtain jobs at the new facility, how long they were unemployed during the conversion effort, or what their pay levels were before and after the conversion. Also missing are data on the number of facilities which simply moved due to enticements at the former bases. Since it sounds like most of the businesses are of this type (the data were accompanied only by newspaper and magazine articles describing a few of these conversions), this would mean that the figures for lost civilian jobs are probably the important ones—i.e., that not only did those workers probably not get the "new" jobs at the bases, but that there probably was only minimal job creation through the conversion process at all.

Estimates of Job Loss

It is impossible to predict with any degree of certainty the overall job loss or job dislocation which will occur due to efforts at cleaning up our environment or in the conversion to a peace-time economy. While we can identify the workers involved in the affected areas, the extent of impact of the measures taken will be determined by the outcome of political battles between the various factions and parties involved on local, state, national, and international levels.

What we can be certain about, however, is that there will be significant dislocation through both conversion and meaningful environmental cleanup. In the latter case though, this may only be an excuse for plant shut-downs or changes that would have occurred anyway.

It is possible, however, to estimate not the number of jobs which will be lost, but the number of workers in the industries which will be most directly affected by environmental cleanup and peace conversion. Within these industries there will almost certainly be disruption and shifts in employment, making workers particularly susceptible to job blackmail tactics by the companies involved.

Table 3 lists the industries which the CONSAD report on jobs at risk from Clean Air Act amendments identifies as potentially "affected" (but in which jobs are not necessarily lost).

Another study of the economic impacts of the acid rain provisions of the Senate and House Bills on the Clean Air Act Amendments (S.1630) points out the number of jobs which might be lost due to the switch from high to low sulfur coals. Northern Appalachia and the Midwest are the major regions producing the high sulfur coals. The study prepared for the U.S. Environmental Protection Agency estimates that as many as 14,000 to 15,000 coal mining jobs might be lost by the year 2000 with 5,000 to 6,000 lost by 1995.[33] The House version of the bill might result in the loss of 6,000 to 7,000 jobs by 1996 and 13,000 to

Table 3
INDUSTRIES TO BE AFFECTED BY
CLEAN AIR ACT AMENDMENTS
Industrial Sector

Leather Products	Misc. Manufacturing
Instruments	Printing/Publishing
Textile Products	Lumber/Wood Products
Fabricated Metals	Food Products
Furniture & Fixtures	Tobacco Products
Rubber/Plastics	Petroleum Refining
Stone/Clay/Concrete	Industrial Machinery
Electronics	Paper Products
Primary Metals	Chemicals
Transportation Equipment	Nitrogen Fertilizer
Industrial Gases	Petroleum Refining
Phosphate Fertilizer	Synthetic Chemicals
Hydraulic Cement	Yarn Spinning Mills
Cylic Crudes	Sawmills
Paperboard Mills	Plastics Materials
Glass Containers	Organic Chemicals
Primary Aluminum	Paper Mills
Inorganic Chemicals	Gray Iron Foundries
Meatpacking Plants	Motor Vehicle Parts
Motor Vehicles	Blast Furnaces/Steel
Misc. Plastics	

Source: Robert W. Hahn and Wilbur Steger, "An Analysis of Jobs-at-Risk and Job Losses Resulting from the Proposed Clean Air Act Amendments," Pittsburgh: CONSAD Research Corporation, Pittsburgh, February 20, 1990, pp. ES7 and ES10.

16,000 by 2001.[34] The study points out that this job loss will not result necessarily in such high numbers of unemployed or dislocated workers since many will be lost through retirement and other "voluntary" reasons, not because their job no longer exists. The study therefore refers to "job slot losses."[35]

There is good reason, moreover, to expect efforts to protect the environment to have even broader impacts. Proposed legislation to ad-

---

Table 4
INDUSTRIES AND JOBS WHICH MAY BE AFFECTED
BY MOVES TO PROTECT THE ENVIRONMENT AND
REDUCE MILITARY PRODUCTION

Industrial Sector	Employment (000s) May 1990
Mining	
Coal Mining	149.7
Oil and Gas Extraction	421.7
Chemical and fertilizer minerals	18.0
Manufacturing	
Lumber and wood products	759.1
Asbestos	9.0
Primary metals industries	766.0
Paper and allied products	695.3
Chemicals and allied products	1,106.2
Petroleum and coal products	166.2
Transportation Equipment	2,078.0

Source: Numbers of employees are from U.S. Department of Labor, Bureau of Labor Statistics, *Employment and Earnings,* July 1990.

---

dress global warming, for example, affects industries from mining and manufacturing to utilities, transportation, and retail and wholesale trade. Efforts to improve the self-reliance of U.S. energy production following the latest Gulf hostilities will likewise affect a broad range of industries, although with conflicting impacts on jobs—efforts at conservation, for example, might have a negative impact, while efforts at increasing coal use or production of other fuel sources might actually erase some of these job losses.[36]

While we cannot predict the numbers of jobs which might be lost or workers dislocated, certainly major portions of the industries listed in Table 4 will be affected by significant changes in environmental standards and military spending.

Hundreds of thousands of additional workers in related service industries (for example, the 130,000 workers in the wholesale trade of chemicals and allied products) will also be affected in greater or lesser measure. The Superfund for Workers is of vital concern to all of these workers and indeed to all Americans who would benefit from cleaning up our environment and demilitarizing our economy.

NOTES

1. U.S. Department of Commerce, *Survey of Current Business,* September issues, 1971 to 1989.
2. Richard Kazis and Richard Grossman, *Fear at Work: Job Blackmail, Labor and the Environment,* New York: Pilgrim Press, 1982.
3. Leonard Woodcock, "Labor and the Economic Impact of Environmental Control Requirements," *Jobs and the Environment: Three Papers,* Berkeley: University of California Institute of Industrial Relations, 1972, p. 5 as cited in Kazis and Grossman, op. cit. pp. 7 and 11.
4. For examples of how the U.S. Forest Service has worked on behalf of the industry, see Jonathan Dushoff, "Razing Alaska: the Destruction of the Tongass Forest," *Multinational Monitor,* July/August 1990, pp. 18-21.
5. John B. Judis, "Ancient Forests, Lost Jobs Ride Wings of Spotted Owl," *In These Times,* August 1-14, 1990.
6. Merry Ann Moore, "Elections 1990," *E Magazine,* September/October 1990, pp. 44-45.
7. "Forest Murder: Ours and Theirs; Tongass Trees Aren't Cheeseburgers," *New York Times,* September 20, 1989.
8. Dirk Johnson, "Wildlife vs. Wage Earner Troubles Taos," *New York Times,* August 14, 1990.
9. Michael Satchell, "Fight for Pigeon River," *U.S. News and World Report,* December 4, 1989, p. 28.
10. Ibid., p. 31.
11. Michael Weaver, "Champion Mill Faces Shutdown," *Asheville Citizen,* January 16, 1989.
12. Millie Buchanan and Gerry Scoppettuolo, "Environment for Cooperation: Building Worker-Community Coalitions," *New Solutions,* Summer 1990.
13. Michael Satchell, op. cit., p. 32.
14. Ibid.
15. Michael Weaver, "Champion Renovation Begins Soon," *Asheville Times,* June 19, 1990.
16. Kit Wagar, "Ashland Oil's Record on Pollution Improving, But

Citations Numerous," *Lexington Herald-Leader,* June 17, 1990.

17. Rick Brady, Proctorville, Ohio, *The Sunday Independent,* May 21, 1989.
18. Irene Taylor, West Virginia, *Huntington Herald Dispatch,* May 28, 1989.
19. Keith Schneider, "Plan Would Revise Farm Subsidies," *New York Times,* October 17, 1990.
20. Robert W. Hahn and Wilbur Steger, "An Analysis of Jobs-at-Risk and Job Losses Resulting from the Proposed Clean Air Act Amendments," Pittsburgh: CONSAD Research Corporation, February 20, 1990, p. ES.15. Emphasis in the original.
21. Advertisement, *New Republic,* May 14, 1990, p. 23.
22. David Wessel, "Air Bill's Cost-Benefit Data Look Very Foggy Up Close," *Wall Street Journal,* May 25, 1990.
23. *Wall Street Journal,* November 22, 1978, as cited in Kazis and Grossman, op. cit., p. 69.
24. Kazis and Grossman, op. cit. Several examples of these exaggerated claims and industry's ability to evade regulations are given.
25. Roger Bezdek et al., "The Economic and Employment Effects of Investments in Pollution Abatement and Control Technologies," *Ambio,* Volume XVIII, No. 5, 1989, pp. 274-279.
26. Management Information Services, Inc., "Numbers of PABCO Jobs Created in 1988," May 1990.
27. Ibid. p. 278.
28. "Permanent Plant Closings, January 1980-May 1986," Oil, Chemical, and Atomic Workers International Union (unpublished).
29. David C. Morrison, "Cushions for Contractors," *National Journal,* January 13, 1990, as cited in Michael Renner, "Swords Into Plowshares: Converting to a Peace Economy," *Worldwatch Paper 96,* June 1990, Washington, DC: Worldwatch Institute, p. 42.
30. As cited in Renner, "Swords into Plowshares," op. cit., p. 42.
31. Toxics Use Reduction and Workers' Health, Series Paper Number 2, "Toxics Use Reduction Case Studies—Impacts on Worker Health and Employment," PIRG Toxics Action Research and Education Project (unpublished draft).
32. Department of Defense, "1961-1986, 25 Years of Civilian Reuse: Summary of Completed Military Base Economic Adjustment Projects," Washington, DC: Department of Defense, April/May 1986.
33. ICF Resources Incorporated, "Comparison of the Economic Im-

pacts of the Acid Rain Provisions of the Senate bill (S.1630) and the House Bill (S.1630)," prepared for the Environmental Protection Agency, July 1990, p. 27.

34. Ibid.

35. Ibid., p. 29. Two paragraphs of this ICF study, in fact, seem to be aimed at heading off job blackmail tactics. The authors note that:

> Despite steadily increasing U.S. coal production since 1970, coal mining employment has shown substantial ups and downs. During most of the 1970s, rapidly declining productivity and rising production led to more than a 50% increase in mining employment. Since the late 1970s, however, average productivity has roughly doubled, leading to a sharp decline in mining employment despite continued increases in production.
>
> Continued gains in coal mining productivity are forecasted for the 1990s and beyond, but at a slower rate of increase than has been seen in the 1980s. As a result, total U.S. coal mining employment is forecasted to exhibit substantially less variation than has been seen over the past two decades, although a further decline in total employment is expected with or without acid rain legislation. (Ibid., p. 27.)

36. However, a study by Management Information Services on the impact of the acid rain provisions of the Clean Air Act finds that the shift from high to low sulphur coal will result in worker dislocation in some regions, but a net increase of over 100,000 jobs overall. Therefore, even in this optimistic scenario, workers in some regions would need to be relocated or retrained for other jobs. (R. M. Wendling and R. H. Bezdek, "Acid Rain Abatement Legislation—Costs and Benefits," *Omega International Journal of Management Science*, Volume 17, No. 3, 1989, pp. 251-261.)

III.

JOBS AND WORK IN THE 1990s: NEW CHALLENGES TO A FAIR DEAL FOR WORKING AMERICANS

American workers are justified in their concern about job loss through efforts to clean up the environment, reduce production and the use of toxics, and demilitarize our economy. The ability of corporations and other environmental polluters (such as operators of military bases, weapons production complexes, and other government-controlled facilities) to argue effectively that environmental cleanup, toxic-use reduction, and military conversion will result in job loss is based on the accurate perception by workers in these industries that they have little chance of finding new jobs comparable to the ones they now hold.

For almost a decade we were treated to rhetoric about the great American job machine that the U.S. economy had become under the Republican administrations of the 1980s. The 18.5 million growth in the number of employed from 1979 to 1989, in fact, represents lackluster growth compared to the previous decade's growth of 20.9 mil-

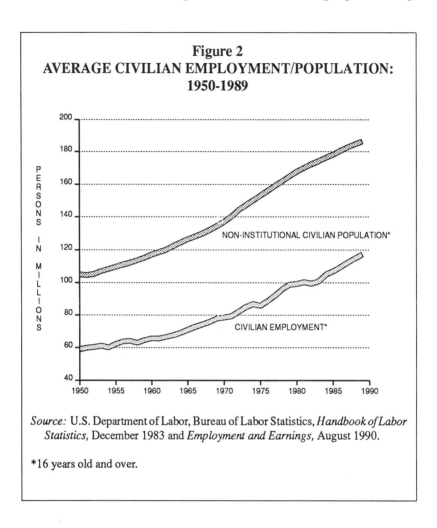

Figure 2
AVERAGE CIVILIAN EMPLOYMENT/POPULATION: 1950-1989

Source: U.S. Department of Labor, Bureau of Labor Statistics, *Handbook of Labor Statistics,* December 1983 and *Employment and Earnings,* August 1990.

*16 years old and over.

lion. As Figure 2 shows, the growth in employment has failed to keep up with the growth in population. (Claims by the Reagan Administration to have created 15.4 million jobs since the 1982 recession could only be made by ignoring the fact that millions of jobs had been lost during that recession.) This growth was only possible due to the proliferation of low-paying, part-time, unskilled, nonunionized jobs in the service sector and was even strong enough to mask the loss of jobs in manufacturing.[1]

Low-Wage Jobs

Since the end of World War II, there has been a steady decline in

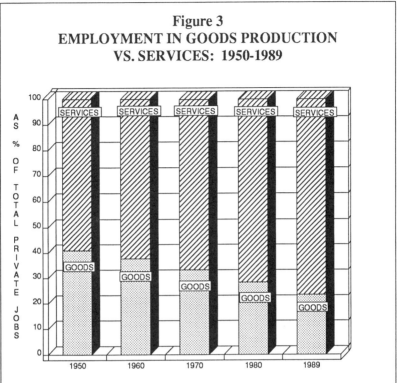

Figure 3
EMPLOYMENT IN GOODS PRODUCTION
VS. SERVICES: 1950-1989

Source: U.S. Department of Labor, Bureau of Labor Statistics, *Employment and Earnings,* August 1990.

the proportion of people in the U.S. labor force involved in the production of goods and a rise in the proportion engaged in the provision of services. This shift has been picking up speed in the last few decades. During the 1960s, there was an 8.2 percent decline in the percentage of workers engaged in production of goods. In the 1970s, that proportion declined by 11.4 percent and in the 1980s, by 16.9 percent. As Figure 3 shows, by 1989 only 23.6 percent of the American workforce was engaged in production of goods—including manufacturing, construction, and mining. Manufacturing now accounts for 18.1 percent of total nonagricultural employment.

This shift in employment to the service sector would not be of such concern were it not for the quality of the jobs being created. Many existing jobs in the service sector are considered to be good jobs. Thus, jobs in the financial sector and in transportation and utilities tend to be

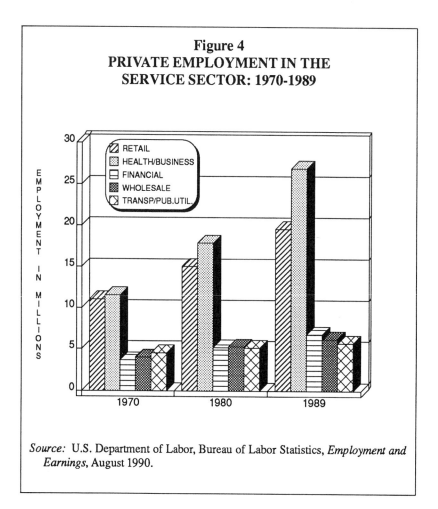

Figure 4
PRIVATE EMPLOYMENT IN THE
SERVICE SECTOR: 1970-1989

Source: U.S. Department of Labor, Bureau of Labor Statistics, *Employment and Earnings*, August 1990.

relatively high-paying and, until recently, seemed to be better from a health and safety perspective. (Recent findings related to repetitive motion injuries and low-level radiation hazards from computer display terminals are causing some concern about the health hazards associated with some of these jobs.) But these are not the sectors where jobs are being created. (In fact, given the recent performance of companies in the financial sector, we can probably expect actual declines in employment in the near future.)

In the last 10 years alone, the number of jobs in retail trade has increased by 4.6 million (see Figure 4). With employment at 19.6 million, retail trade now accounts for 18 percent of total employment in the U.S. economy and, as of September 1989, there are now more employees in retail trade than in the manufacturing sector.

Jobs in the health and business services have grown even faster. In 1989, such jobs accounted for 24.8 percent of all jobs, up from 19.1 percent 10 years ago and 15.9 percent in 1969. In all, 77 percent of net job creation over the last 10 years has been in retail trade and health and business services. So why worry? Because these two sectors pay the lowest wages in the U.S. economy.

In June 1990, jobs in retail trade paid an average hourly wage of $6.77, and jobs in health and business services paid $9.73 per hour. These wages are 68.0 percent and 98.0 percent, respectively, of hourly wages of total private employment, and 62.6 percent and 89.9 percent of hourly wages in manufacturing. While jobs in transportation and public utilities pay average hourly wages above those in manufacturing ($12.81 compared with $10.82 in manufacturing) and those in finance, insurance and real estate only slightly below ($9.88), these two sectors together only account for 11.6 percent of total employment and only 12.8 percent of net job growth in the last decade.

Part-Time Employment

But hourly wages tell only part of the story. The new jobs in the service sector are also often part time. Workers in the manufacturing sector, for example, work an average of 41 hours a week and those in mining work 43 hours a week. Overall, the average work week for Americans is 35 hours.

But in the fastest-growing sectors of our economy, the average worker is only employed for 29 hours in retail trade and 33 hours in health and business services. This results in average weekly wages of $189 and $306 respectively, compared with $429 in manufacturing and $562 in mining. Thus, *weekly* wages in retail trade are only 44.1 percent of those in manufacturing and a mere 33.6 percent of mining, an area of employment likely to be hard hit by environmental cleanup. The comparable figures for health and business services are 71.3 percent and 54.4 percent of manufacturing and mining. Figure 5 shows that these discrepancies have grown over the last thirty years.

As a result, one job is often insufficient to support an individual, let alone a family. Therefore, we have witnessed both an increase in the number of people holding jobs but living below the poverty level,[2] and a growth in the number of families supported by more than one worker.

These trends are not just statistical abstractions. Their impacts are being felt in the decline in real purchasing power of weekly wages and

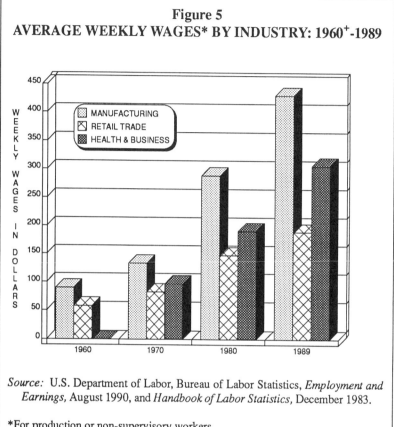

Figure 5
AVERAGE WEEKLY WAGES* BY INDUSTRY: 1960[+]-1989

Source: U.S. Department of Labor, Bureau of Labor Statistics, *Employment and Earnings,* August 1990, and *Handbook of Labor Statistics,* December 1983.

*For production or non-supervisory workers.

[+]Health and business data for 1960 not available.

in a concurrent rise in the number of Americans living in poverty. The real wage, adjusted for inflation, of the "average" American worker has fallen to 83.9 percent of its level in 1972 (see Figure 6). The downward trend is especially evident in the service sector, but also in manufacturing, where a decline in unionization and in the relative bargaining power of workers has led to a drop in real wages so that they are now lower than during any year since 1961.

Increasing Joblessness

So the Great American Job Machine is not grinding out high-paying

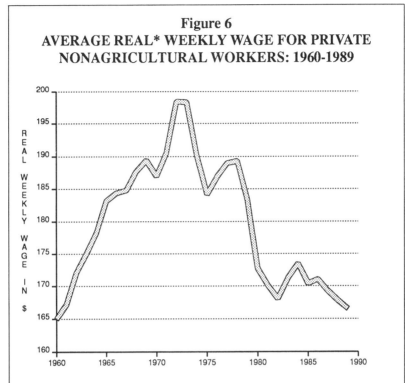

Figure 6
AVERAGE REAL* WEEKLY WAGE FOR PRIVATE NONAGRICULTURAL WORKERS: 1960-1989

Source: U.S. Department of Labor, Bureau of Labor Statistics, *Supplement to Employment and Earnings,* August 1981, July 1984, June 1985, August 1989; and *Employment and Earnings,* March 1990.

*In 1977 dollars for production or nonsupervisory workers.

jobs for workers to step into when they lose their existing jobs due to military restructuring, environmental cleanup, and toxic-use reduction. In fact, it is not doing very well in keeping pace with the current workforce. This situation is effectively concealed by the way the official unemployment rate is calculated. Thus, the Bureau of Labor Statistics, which produces the monthly unemployment rate, counts a person as fully employed if he or she has worked as little as *one* hour in a week. In a similar distorting manner, the Bureau of Labor Statistics counts people as unemployed only if they are out of a job and have been actively seeking work during the preceding four weeks. As the length of time it takes to find new employment increases, a growing number of workers fall out of the official labor force altogether. The result of these

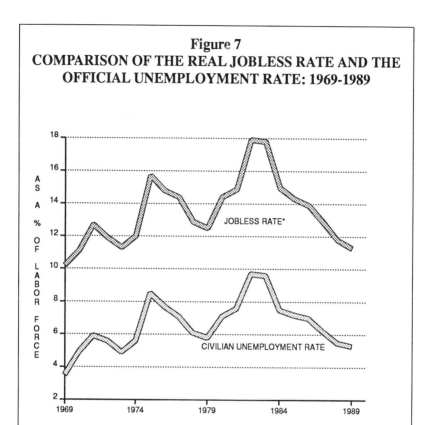

Figure 7
COMPARISON OF THE REAL JOBLESS RATE AND THE OFFICIAL UNEMPLOYMENT RATE: 1969-1989

Source: Analysis based on U.S. Department of Labor, Bureau of Labor Statistics, *Employment and Earnings,* January 1970-January 1990.

*For further information on the jobless rate, see David Dembo and Ward Morehouse, *Underbelly of the U.S. Economy: Joblessness and Pauperization of Work in America,* Council on International and Public Affairs, New York, November 1988.

distortions is that the number of jobless persons now stands at 13.7 million people—a jobless rate of 11.3 percent, more than twice the 5.3 percent "official" unemployment rate the government would have us believe.

Full employment, the stated goal of many politicians, and one of the justifications for our economic system, is a less and less likely prospect for our economy. As Figure 7 shows, the number of officially unemployed has risen steadily over the last several decades, and "acceptable" levels of unemployment have risen as well. Following the dismal record of unemployment in the late 1970s and 1980s, five percent seems to have become an acceptable level. This abstract percentage, however, translates to 6.4 million persons looking for work and potentially in competition with those laid off due to actions taken to address environmental pollution prevention and cleanup as well as demilitarization of the economy.

But, the official unemployment rate is roughly half of the real jobless rate, with large numbers of part-time workers and people who have just given up looking for work excluded from the government's definition of "unemployed." Workers in the industries where major job losses will occur, as efforts to clean up and demilitarize our society accelerate, face an economy where joblessness is at historically high levels during both recessions and recoveries and the majority of new jobs will not pay wages high enough to support these workers or their families.

Displaced Workers

The fact that more and more jobs are part time and/or low-paying coincides with a rise in the two-worker household—a consequence in part of the inability of one worker to support a family. But workers who lose their jobs due to cutbacks and closings of industrial plants face hardships in addition to the nonexistence of jobs comparable to those they have lost. They typically do not have skills matched to available jobs, live in areas where new jobs are unavailable, are too old or too young to be among the top contenders for such jobs, and, employed in the hazardous industries with which we are concerned, have often been poisoned or injured in the jobs they have lost.

Recent studies of so-called "discouraged" or "dislocated" workers by the Bureau of Labor Statistics and the U.S. Congressional Office of Technology Assessment[3] provide insights into the difficulties likely to be encountered by workers who lose their jobs in manufacturing, mining, or other industries because of efforts to clean up the environment, reduce the use and production of toxics, and demilitarize our economy.

Following the 1982 to 1983 recession, the Bureau of Labor Statistics began releasing periodic reports on the experiences of workers who lost jobs due to "plant closing, moving of plants or businesses, elimination of individual jobs or complete shifts, or 'slack work.'" Since the Labor Department historically tends to be interested primarily in established workers (those with "strong ties to the labor force"), the studies, while pointing to the large numbers of workers who lost jobs (11 million during the recession, for example), focus on those who had held their jobs for three or more years. Thus, the Bureau of Labor Statistics ignores the millions of workers who often had fewer skills and less experience.

But even so, the difficulty these "mainstream" workers have in finding new jobs, and especially jobs with comparable pay levels, is illuminating. From January 1979 to January 1984, 5.1 million workers lost jobs they had held for three or more years. Of these, only 1.2 million were reemployed within five weeks. Over 1.2 million were still jobless one year after losing their jobs.

Of those who lost full-time jobs and were rehired (2 million), 54 percent found jobs which paid the same or more than the job they lost. Thirty percent were only able to find jobs at 20 percent or more below their previous wage (see Figure 8). And for workers in manufacturing occupations, 53 percent were able to find jobs only below their former wage.

Displacement was especially hard on manufacturing workers. Not only were half of all displaced workers from 1979 to 1984 in the manufacturing sector, but only 58 percent of these workers were able to find new jobs by the time of the study. A study of displaced workers by the U.S. Congressional Office of Technology Assessment found that "production workers—skilled, semiskilled, and unskilled—lost jobs in far greater proportion to their numbers than managers, professionals and technicians."[4]

In the more recent study (4.7 million workers who lost jobs from January 1983 through January 1988), 71.4 percent were able to find another job by January 1988. Of the 3.2 million who lost full time jobs and were reemployed by January 1988, 306,000 found only part time jobs. Another 1.1 million were only able to find jobs which paid below their previous wage level (see Figure 9).

Elderly, black, Hispanic, and female workers suffered disproportionately. Only 50.7 percent of those over 55 were reemployed (in contrast to 71 percent for those 20 years and over). Comparable figures are 66.4 percent for women (74.2 percent for men), 65.0 percent for blacks, and 66.6 percent for Hispanics (72.4 percent for whites).

It is clear that the U.S. economy is not creating the kinds of jobs needed to support millions of Americans at decent levels. Equally evident is the fact that we can no longer continue to create jobs dependent on the destruction of our environment. With the millions of workers

Figure 8
JOB STATUS IN JANUARY 1984 OF
11.5 MILLION WORKERS WHO LOST JOBS
FROM JANUARY 1979 TO JANUARY 1984

KEY:

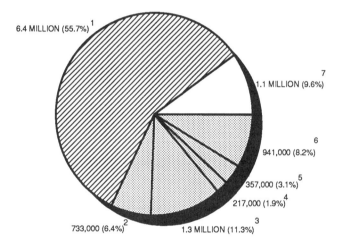

6.4 MILLION (55.7%) [1]

1.1 MILLION (9.6%) [7]

941,000 (8.2%) [6]

357,000 (3.1%) [5]

217,000 (1.9%) [4]

1.3 MILLION (11.3%) [3]

733,000 (6.4%) [2]

Source: Paul O. Flain and Ellen Sehgal, "Displaced Workers of 1979-1983: How Well Have They Fared?" *Monthly Labor Review,* June 1985.

1. These workers held their jobs for fewer than three years when they were laid off and were not of interest to the Bureau of Labor Statistics.
2. These workers dropped out of the labor force (i.e. stopped looking for work altogether).
3. These workers were still unemployed at the time of the study.
4. These workers were reemployed but data on wages is unavailable.
5. These workers could only find part-time employment.
6. These workers could only find jobs that paid less than their previous jobs.
7. These workers found jobs at or above their previous wages.

Note: Percentages may not add up to 100 due to rounding.

Figure 9
JOB STATUS IN JANUARY 1988 OF
9.7 MILLION WORKERS WHO LOST JOBS
FROM JANUARY 1983 TO JANUARY 1988

KEY:

 Workers unable to find new full-time jobs paying the same or more than their old jobs.

Workers who held jobs fewer than three years.

Workers who found jobs at or above their previous wage.

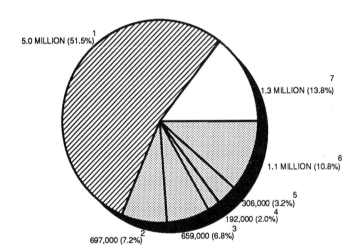

5.0 MILLION (51.5%)¹

7
1.3 MILLION (13.8%)

6
1.1 MILLION (10.8%)

5
306,000 (3.2%)
4
192,000 (2.0%)
3
659,000 (6.8%)
2
697,000 (7.2%)

Source: U.S. Department of Labor, Bureau of Labor Statistics, "BLS Reports on Worker Displacement," *Press Release,* December 9, 1988.

1. These workers held jobs fewer than three years when they were laid off and were not included in study.
2. These workers dropped out of the labor force.
3. These workers were still unemployed.
4. Data on wages for these workers is unavailable.
5. These workers could only find part-time jobs.
6. These workers could only find jobs paying below their former wages.
7. These workers found jobs paying at or above their previous wages.

Note: Percentages may not add up to 100 due to rounding.

who are already displaced and jobless, it is crucial that we begin to look at the changing nature of work and the relationship between work and income from new perspectives. The Superfund for Workers provides a means for moving forward, both in cleaning up our environment and reducing pollutants, as well as providing a new tool for workers to adapt and take part in the fundamental changes taking place in the economy which we have outlined above.

NOTES

1. Data are from Department of Labor, Bureau of Labor Statistics, *Employment and Earnings,* Washington, DC: U.S. Government Printing Office, January 1990. All data on job losses, new jobs, trends in employment, and wage levels in this chapter are from the Bureau of Labor Statistics, *Employment and Earnings,* Washington, DC: U.S. Government Printing Office, and the *Supplement to Employment and Earnings,* various issues.
2. From 1980 to 1987, the total number of persons living below the poverty level who work increased from 7.8 million to 8.4 million. (U.S. Department of Commerce, Bureau of the Census, "Money Income and Poverty Status of Families and Persons in the United States: 1986 and 1987," *Current Population Reports, Series P-60,* Washington, DC: U.S. Government Printing Office, 1987 and 1988.)
3. U.S. Congress, Office of Technology Assessment, *Technology and Structural Unemployment: Reemploying Displaced Adults,* (OTA-ITE-250), Washington, DC: U.S. Government Printing Office, February 1986, p. 109.
4. This section is based on Paul O. Flaim and Ellen Sehgal, "Displaced Workers of 1979-1983: How Well Have They Fared?" *Monthly Labor Review,* June 1985; "BLS Reports on Worker Displacement," *BLS News Release,* December 9, 1988; and *Technology and Structural Unemployment,* op. cit.

IV.

PRECEDENTS TO THE SUPERFUND

Educational assistance and retraining for the unemployed, in particular dislocated workers, is hardly a new idea. Several programs have provided such assistance in the past. The most relevant to the Superfund is the GI Bill which emphasized the importance of education in retraining and relocating veterans and war industry workers after the Second World War.

The GI Bill was the only initiative which provided meaningful choices to unemployed people in the future conduct of their own lives. It was thus a tool of empowerment to such people, unlike other efforts described below which were and are inadequate for workers who still end up bearing most of the burden of economic change and reap precious little of the benefit.

Trade Adjustment Assistance and the Job Training Partnership Act provide workers affected by government trade policies with aid. However, these programs are marginal and inadequate and do little to address the real concerns of working people in a society characterized by great and, since 1980, rapidly increasing concentrations of wealth and the economic and political power that goes with it. The rationale behind this assistance is that workers who bear the greatest cost in terms of lost jobs or income due to trade policies, which are supposed to benefit the majority of the population (and certainly do benefit a few), are entitled to special assistance.

Proposals have also been made to amend recent legislation that could result in job loss to include help to affected working populations on the grounds that they alone should not bear the costs of environmental pollution prevention and cleanup or peace initiatives, which in theory should benefit everyone. We examine several of these programs and their provisions in order to gain a clearer understanding of the concept of a Superfund for Workers as an initiative in public policy.

The GI Bill

Provision of aid to both unemployed veterans and dislocated workers, with emphasis on educational assistance, was suggested as early as 1919 in the United States. In the aftermath of the First World War, four million servicemen were demobilized within one year with only a one-time $60 severance payment. At the same time, thousands of workers lost their jobs in the transition from a war to a peacetime economy with no unemployment compensation. The resulting unemployment and disaffection of workers posed a crisis to the economy.[1]

By contrast, following World War I, Great Britain did make preparations for releasing servicemen into civilian life, as well as for war workers who were dislocated. The program covered 5 million servicemen and millions of civilian workers. The plan provided apprenticeship training and focused on educational assistance.[2]

The U.S. learned from the experience of the First World War the importance of making preparations to convert from a war to a peacetime economy. Eleven million veterans had to make the transition to civilian life after World War II, and nearly half of the labor force was affected.[3]

Several steps led to the passage of the original GI Bill in 1944. There was grave concern over possible violence at the end of World War II if no plans were made to incorporate veterans and war-related workers into the civilian economy. One suggestion was to retain men in service until they had secured employment, as the British had done after World War I (which was also cheaper than dealing with unemployment-imposed depression).[4]

In 1942, the Commission on Post-War Training and Adjustment, also known as the Columbia University Committee, was formed by the Adult Education Institute of Columbia University to address the issue of conversion and financial assistance to veterans. The Committee was composed of 45 leading academics who examined adult education as a means of relocating veterans after the war. The Committee concluded that war workers should be included in the program as well. It recommended that local control be exercised over the program as much as possible due to a fear of governmental interference in education. From the beginning, it was made clear that the Federal Government would be responsible for financing the program for servicemen (and to a lesser degree for workers).[5]

In 1942, President Roosevelt signed the Selective Service Act and appointed the Armed Forces Services Committee on Post-War Educational Opportunities for Service Personnel, made up of educators, to study interrupted educations in relation to veterans. The Committee, referred to as the Osborne Committee after its chairperson Brigadier General Frederick Osborne, drew up guidelines which laid the foundation for the GI Bill. It recommended that the Federal Government provide a maximum of one year of education and training benefits to every person who had served six or more months in the armed forces since 1940, to begin not more than six months after leaving service. This provided veterans with the opportunity to retrain for civilian jobs, or to continue their education in cases where it was interrupted by the war. Both vocational and university training were offered, with freedom of choice of institution and subject area. The Osborne Committee also recommended that the Federal Government extend educational assistance to workers displaced due to demobilization.[6]

The result of these previous efforts was the Servicemen's Readjustment Act of 1944 (the first GI Bill), which entitled veterans to one year of educational assistance plus a year of education for each additional year of service (up to four years). Financial aid included tuition and fees, plus a monthly allowance.[7] War industry workers were not covered by the legislation, however. This came at a time (1944-1948) when the Gross Federal Debt of the United States actually exceeded the Gross National Product (GNP), the only time this has been the case since 1940. The Federal deficit at that time (1946) was also far worse proportionately (at 7.5 percent of GNP) than it is now. In 1989, the U.S. Federal Debt was 55.6 percent and the federal deficit was 3.0 percent of the GNP.[8]

The Veterans Readjustment Assistance Act of 1952 (the Korean GI Bill) extended economic benefits to Korean veterans in an effort to minimize serious unemployment, and succeeded in correcting some of the shortcomings of the first GI Bill. Payments were made directly to veterans (rather than to schools) to guard against abuses of the Act. Tuition and fees as well as a monthly allowance (adjusted for each additional dependent) were included in the payments. Veterans had to submit proof of enrollment, and demonstrate satisfactory progress in order to receive payments. In addition to educational benefits, the Korean GI Bill included loan guarantees, employment assistance, unemployment compensation, and severance payments.[9] Education and training benefits were equal to 1.5 times the length of service, with a ceiling at 36 months of benefits. Some 2.4 million former military personnel participated in the program.[10]

The Veterans' Readjustment Benefits Act of 1966 (the "Cold War GI Bill") passed despite opposition due to its cost. The Act provided both education and housing benefits. Estimated costs of the program were between $325 to $400 million per year, and covered approximately 5.5 million veterans who served between 1955 and July, 1967. The bill provided one month of educational assistance (rather than 1.5) for each month of service, up to a maximum of 36 months. It did not provide on-the-job training or job counseling as the Korean Bill had done. The bill was permanent in nature, however.[11]

Changes were made in the Cold War Bill in 1968-1969 to include on-the-job training (which required employers to pay wages no less than those paid to nonveterans), predischarge educational programs, courses to correct academic deficiencies, and a relaxation of minimum course hour requirements. On-the-job training was funded only in instances where there was reasonable assurance that training would lead to employment. Only 10 percent of veterans opted for on-the-job training or an apprenticeship. In 1972, further changes were made which established limitations on educational benefits at 75 percent of tuition and fees or $1,000, whichever was less. Calls for greater emphasis on apprenticeships and an increase in entitlements to 48 months were made. A work/study program was also established for veterans.[12]

A total of 13.5 million veterans participated in the education and training programs between 1945 and 1972 at a cost of over $24.6 billion.[13]

Trade Adjustment Assistance

The Trade Expansion Act was passed in 1962 to aid workers and businesses hurt by the nation's trade policy, which lowered trade barriers to foreign imports. The rationale behind the Act was that people who bear the heaviest costs of the nation's free trade policies deserve special assistance. The Act was intended as aid to adjustment, but was so restrictive in terms of eligibility requirements that no one qualified between 1962 and 1969.[14] In fact, in the first twelve years, only 35,000 workers received assistance from the Trade Act. Therefore, the program was reorganized in the Trade Act of 1974.[15]

To be eligible for Trade Adjustment Assistance (TAA) benefits as of 1974, a worker must be laid off or threatened with a layoff; a significant number of workers in the firm must have lost their jobs or be threatened with such loss; sales must have decreased; and imports must have contributed to job loss and decline of sales. However, workers no longer had to prove that imports were a major cause of the adversity to firms and workers, but only "contributed importantly." The relaxation of eligibility requirements was the most important feature of the 1974 revisions. The benefits were established in 1974 at 70 percent of the worker's weekly wage, paid weekly. It provided a maximum of 18 months of income support.

The major aim of the TAA legislation is to train workers in new skills, but it also provides income support, out-of-area job search, counseling and placement services, and relocation assistance. Workers are eligible for income support (combined with unemployment insurance) for up to 75 percent of their previous wage for a maximum of one year of unemployment.[16]

Expenditures and the number of workers served under TAA legislation peaked in 1980 at $1.6 billion and 532,000 workers served before eligibility was tightened under the Reagan/Bush administration.[17] Training and relocation assistance have made up only about 25 percent of TAA spending since 1982, as the program was severely cut back in 1981. Under the new, tighter regulations, both money spent and the number of recipients dropped. Instead, the program became more of a source for long-term income support, even for workers not in the training program. In addition, income support under TAA was cut back to 50 percent of the previous weekly wage, and eligibility requirements were stiffened. The program was extended in 1986 until 1991.[18]

The Job Training Partnership Act (JTPA) replaced the Comprehensive Employment and Training Act when it was up for renewal in 1982. JTPA was the Reagan administration's weakened version of CETA. Unlike JTPA, CETA grants included funds for public service employment as well as training. Funds were considerably larger under CETA than JTPA. Federal appropriations for JTPA in 1984 to 1985 for Title III were $221 million compared with over $9 billion for CETA in its peak year.[19] JTPA is open to experienced (three or more years on-the-job) workers who lose their job when U.S. industries close plants, automate, or move operations overseas. Seventy percent of funds are devoted to training activities, and it is administered at the state level. Unlike the Trade Adjustment Assistance act where workers have to wait at least 60 days for approval, an immediate response is available under Title III of the Job Training Partnership Act.[20] The program suffered a severe cutback from $223 million for 1985 to $96 million in 1986.[21]

Between July 1984 and June 1987, JTPA served approximately 386,000 people[22]—only a small portion of the annual average of 1 million workers who were displaced from full-time jobs they had held for more than three years during this period. As indicated in Chapter III, there were actually 9.7 million workers over the age of 20 who were displaced between 1983 and 1988.[23]

In 1987, Trade Adjustment Assistance funds began to run out. In 1988, a comprehensive program was proposed that would combine Title III with TAA and other programs. The program was called the Trade, Employment and Productivity Act of 1987. The Act incorporates TAA features plus new ones, such as rapid state response to plant closings and large layoffs. The Act called for $980 million in funding in 1987, as opposed to the $223 million in 1987 for the Job Training Partnership Act and $206 million for TAA, and would allow up to two years of training, but provides no extended income support. The Act is designed to be coordinated with the Job Training Partnership Act and to serve as an additional source of aid once other resources have been exhausted (such as unemployment compensation). The Act was passed into law as part of the Omnibus Trade and Competitiveness Act of 1988.[24]

Recent Programs for Displaced Workers

Clean Air Act Amendments

The Superfund for Workers is not the only program which has been proposed to address workers whose jobs are in jeopardy due to environmental and peace initiatives. During recent debates over the reauthorization of the Clean Air Act, proposals have been submitted by members of Congress, although clearly as an afterthought as there were no transition provisions in the original Bill, to provide for workers who would lose their jobs, primarily as a result of acid rain provisions to reduce coal-burning emissions.

Because the Clean Air Act will almost certainly result in the closing of some of the higher sulphur content coal mines in this country, there have been efforts, however small, to protect coal miners in the hardest-hit areas. Amendments to the Clean Air Act proposed by Senator Byrd and Representative Bob Wise, both of West Virginia, opened up national discussion for a brief period on the need to address these issues.

The purpose of the amendment proposed by Senator Byrd, entitled the "Relief for Terminated Workers Act," was "to help minimize the effects on workers who are terminated from their employment as a result of the Clean Air Act Amendments of 1990."

The Act would have provided for three years of "termination benefits" to be paid to coal mine workers who lose their jobs as a direct result of the Clean Air Act Amendments. The benefits, according to the Act, were to be 70 percent of a worker's wage for the first year, 60 percent for the second year, and 50 percent for the third year.

The Byrd amendment did include a very modest provision for retraining and education under the proposed amendment:

> At any time during the 3-year period ... any terminated coal mine worker or eligible terminated employee while engaged in a full-time retraining or educational program certified by the Secretary [of Labor], after consultation with the appropriate Committees of Congress, as appropriate for purposes of this title, shall, while satisfactorily participating, receive, in addition to the benefit under section 605, an amount, not to exceed in the aggregate, $4,000 for a period not to exceed 12 months.

Despite estimates that 5,000 miners might lose their jobs because of the acid rain provisions of the Clean Air Act Amendments, Byrd's amendment failed by one vote in the Senate.[25]

Representative Bob Wise's more restrictive amendment to the Clean Air Act passed the House on May 23, 1990. The amendment is entitled "The Clean Air Employment Transition Assistance." It provides for only one year of benefits, and is designed to complement unemployment insurance and the Job Training Partnership Act. The Act amends the Job Training Partnership Act to include workers adversely affected due to company compliance with the Clean Air Act. Allowances under the amendment for 1992 are $30 million. No on-the-job training is available, nor are there education benefits with the exception of education that is necessary in order to obtain skills needed for a particular position.

The version of the Clean Air Act that was adopted includes a provision of $250 million for unemployment and retraining benefits for workers who lose their jobs because of the new law.[26]

Defense Economic Adjustment Act
(H.R. 101)

This bill, first introduced by Representative Ted Weiss of New York in 1977, outlines a strategy for military conversion. In the face of military cutbacks after the defense industry's boom in the 1980s, the legislation is once again up for consideration. The bill calls for a Defense Economic Adjustment Council to prepare guidelines for conversion. It also requires that every military base, production facility, and laboratory engaged in military research with more than 100 employees establish future alternative use plans as a prerequisite for obtaining future military contracts. The bill states that the Secretary of Defense is required to give one year's advance notice of any layoffs.

The Defense Economic Adjustment Act has provisions for occupational retraining of displaced military industry employees as well as income support and relocation allowances. A national job-search network would also be created. Communities "seriously affected" by military spending reductions would "be eligible for Federal assistance for planning for economic adjustment to avoid substantial dislocations." The program would be financed by a fund which would receive 10 percent of any savings in defense spending.[27]

Each of the programs discussed here provides examples of efforts to help workers dislocated through shifts in public policy. But they also illustrate (with the exception of the original GI Bill) the inadequacies of such efforts to address the real underlying concerns of displaced workers and to provide these workers with meaningful and truly empowering choices in their lives. That is what we believe the Superfund for Workers as outlined in the next chapter would do.

NOTES

1. Theodore R. Mosch, *The GI Bill: A Breakthrough in Educational and Social Policy in the United States,* Hicksville, N.Y.: Exposition Press, 1975, p. 14.
2. Ibid., pp. 18-19.
3. Ibid., p. 20.
4. Ibid., p. 21.

5. Ibid., pp. 26-27.
6. Ibid., pp. 27-31.
7. Ibid., pp. 38-39.
8. Executive Office of the President, Office of Management and Budget, *Budget of the United States Government, 1991*, Washington, DC: U.S. Government Printing Office, 1990.
9. Ibid., pp. 49-51.
10. Sar Levitan and Joyce Zickler, *Swords Into Plowshares: Our GI Bill*, Salt Lake City: Olympus Publishing Company, 1973, pp. 38, 42.
11. Mosch, op. cit., pp. 59, 62-64.
12. Ibid., pp. 75-81.
13. Levitan and Zickler, op. cit., p. 38.
14. U.S. Congress, Office of Technology Assessment, *Trade Adjustment Assistance: New Ideas for an Old Program*, Washington, DC: Office of Technology Assessment, June 1987, pp. 20-22.
15. Duane Leigh, *Assisting Displaced Workers: Do the States Have A Better Idea?*, Washington, DC: W.E. Upjohn Institute for Employment Research, 1989, p. 21.
16. Office of Technology Assessment, *Trade Adjustment Assistance,* op. cit., pp. 22-23.
17. Leigh, p. 21.
18. Ibid., p. 22.
19. Ibid.
20. Office of Technology Assessment, *Trade Adjustment Assistance,* op. cit., p. 9.
21. Leigh, p. 23.
22. Adam Seitchik and Jeffrey Zornitsky, *From One Job to the Next: Workers Adjustment in a Changing Labor Market,* Washington, DC: W.E. Upjohn Institute for Employment Research, 1989, p.5.
23. "BLS Reports on Worker Displacement," *BLS News Release,* December 9, 1988.
24. Leigh, op. cit., pp. 3, 23.
25. Richard Berke, "House Clears the Way for Passage of a Strengthened Clean Air Act," *New York Times,* May 24, 1990.
26. "Lawmakers Reach Accord on Clean Air," *New York Times,* October 23, 1990; "Bush Signs Major Revision of Anti-Pollution Law," *New York Times,* November 16, 1990.
27. Michael Renner, "Swords Into Plowshares: Converting to a Peace Economy," *Worldwatch Paper 96,* Washington, DC: Worldwatch Institute, June 1990, pp. 59-60.

V.

NEW CAREERS FOR WORKING AMERICANS: THE SUPERFUND FOR DISPLACED WORKERS

The Predicament of Displaced Workers: Inadequate, Irrelevant, or Inappropriate Remedies

Many Americans now recognize that we must move quickly and with a much more substantial effort than in the past not only to clean up our environment but to reduce sharply our use of toxic chemicals. There is, of course, some disagreement about how this should be done and who should pay. But about the overall need there is broad consensus, even though there is little understanding of the extent of change necessary to achieve true environmental sustainability.[1]

Unfortunately, the U.S. economy is heavily dependent on toxic production. In states like California, Louisiana, Texas, and New Jersey, a substantial proportion of all manufacturing jobs and corporate profits are toxic-dependent. These hazardous jobs are often among the highest paying for blue-collar workers.

As workers, communities, and even our government move forward with environmental cleanup, conflicts are inevitable because the future job security of workers in these industries will be in jeopardy. What kinds of responses are made to prospective displaced workers when they ask about their future? Here are five, all inadequate, irrelevant, or inappropriate:

1. "Your plant is not closing because it produces toxics but because it is no longer profitable." This kind of statement is difficult to prove and certainly offers little comfort to workers losing their jobs.

2. "If we all—the company, the workers, the community—work together, we can both save your job and clean up the environment." But many jobs will have to go because our environmental problems have become so severe that merely cleaning up after the mess has been created will no longer do. We must sharply reduce the volume and type of toxics that we produce and use.

3. "There are more jobs created in the pollution control industry than are lost in the toxic industry." If this were true—and with increasing emphasis for the future on reduction of toxic production and use rather than cleanup, this will be less and less so—how do impacted workers from toxic industries get those new jobs? Where are they? Will the displaced workers be forced to move, disrupt their family and community life, and work for lower pay somewhere else?

   Is it even reasonable to expect workers from toxic industries to seek jobs in the pollution control industry? Many of these jobs are dirty and disagreeable—and involve continued exposure to health and safety hazards in the work place. In fact, most of the jobs that have been created in pollution control, as Table 2 in Chapter II shows, are janitorial or clerical. Toxic workers have already borne a disproportionate share of risk. They deserve a safer environment for the rest of their working lives.

4. "You can get retrained for alternative jobs." This is a cruel hoax. Very few jobs at comparable pay in industrial production exist for these displaced workers, as we have demonstrated in Chapter III. Most

retraining programs are short-term and geared to dead-end, low-skill jobs at much lower pay. And what are workers and families to live on if they seek a fundamentally different career through long-term education?

5. "We can convert the facility to nontoxic production and save the jobs." This is certainly a noble objective but raises some difficult questions. How long would it take? Would the employment be stable? Could we be sure that it will require the same number and types of workers and will have the same wages? Such conversions are clearly desirable if they will help to minimize adverse economic impact on local communities that plant closings often entail, but it is quite unlikely that these conversions will retain all of the workers in the old plant on the job at comparable pay.

Each of these responses to prospective displaced workers is flawed. Lacking is immediate assured help that will enable displaced workers to move on to other careers without reducing their existing standard of living and causing great stress to themselves and their families. What we need is a program that addresses this economic reality for displaced workers.

Industrial workers are facing a number of obstacles to their ability to make a living. Concurrently with the first efforts at cleaning up America by closing down or drastically reducing America's most polluting industries, the end of the Cold War is reducing defense spending.

This will simultaneously accelerate environmental cleanup efforts since much defense production is also highly polluting—for example, nuclear weapons plants. Cutbacks in defense production are hitting blue-collar industrial workers hard, causing personal anguish and community devastation by the loss of defense-related production.

We are dealing not only with abstract numbers such as the projected job loss in different industries presented in Chapter II, but also with human lives that are being disrupted and drastically impacted with pain, suffering, and uncertainty. While some of those affected are white male blue-collar industrial workers (whose frequent middle-aged status will make finding a comparable job all the tougher), many are women or minority workers for whom the loss of a decent-paying industrial job will mean disaster to them and their families. Consider Gail Sibley, a single mother with a six-year-old asthmatic son, who was laid off from her $31,000 a year job at the United Nuclear Corporation's defense plant in Montville, Connecticut, last March. Or take the case of Vivian Rowden, a 46-year-old dispatcher at Lockheed Aeronautical Systems Company Plant in Burbank, California who lost her job in June and who is responsible for supporting a disabled husband, a son, and her elderly mother on her $16 per hour pay.[2]

On top of all this, industrial workers are put into the position of having to defend the products they are making even though they have no say in the choice of those products and the way they are made. This they must do because, their employers insist, their own security and that of their families is at stake.

The Superfund Program

The Superfund for Workers will provide those displaced from environmentally destructive or military industries with four years of support for further education and/or training at an institution of their own choosing. Full tuition and compensation support will be provided at the average union wage in the geographical region and industrial sector in which they were employed, provided they are enrolled full time in an educational or equivalent program. They will continue to receive the same or similar fringe benefits, including health insurance and child care support.

Workers will choose the educational or training program that best serves their needs within broad guidelines that would assure that they are preparing themselves for useful and fulfilling roles in society. It might involve a relatively short period of retraining with a specific vocational objective in view. But it would also provide the option for a fundamental shift in careers that would be possible only through an extended program of study, earning a college degree or some form of professional or technical certification. The changing character of work in our society and continuing need for environmental cleanup, toxic use reduction, and conversion to an economy less dependent on military production will give displaced workers a strong incentive to choose an option that would prepare them for a new career and empower them to shape their future working lives.

At the completion of four years of further education or training, workers would seek employment in their new careers for which job counseling, career placement and relocation services will be provided under the Superfund program. For middle-aged or older workers, locating a new job poses special difficulties. There might be an option of continuing at a reduced level of compensation under the program until a stipulated retirement age while engaged in community or social service with a nonprofit organization or local government agency, which would also provide a portion of their wages and benefits (much as the federally subsidized work-study program for college students now does).

This option is but one of many features of the Superfund for Workers that should be debated as consideration of the basic concept moves forward.

Alternatives to College

There are a number of possible variations on the basic plan. For example, if workers had an option of being employed part time at their existing jobs, they might go to school part time, with the balance of their compensation at the average wage in their industry coming from the Superfund for Workers. Yet another possible variation—if a worker participating in the program wanted to become a craftsman—would be a period of apprenticeship to a recognized master of that particular craft. Such apprenticeships sometimes carry a small stipend, which would be deducted from compensation provided by the Superfund for Workers. This pattern is already well established in public policy through cooperative work/study programs of various kinds.

Still other variations include different forms of on-the-job training in a new career, preparation for and seed money to help start a small business, or early retirement at a reduced level of compensation.

We recognize that not all workers eligible for the Superfund will be academically equipped or will want to carry on a regular program of college study. That is why we urge that the other options suggested above be available. If workers do elect to go to college, they should be treated as "non-traditional" students and given the opportunity to design their own course of study as a form of individualized "contract learning," a practice already widely followed in college and university programs for older students. Such programs also typically give credit for relevant work and life experience.

We recognize as well that some colleges and universities will try to take advantage of workers coming to them through the Superfund and some workers will attempt to rip off the Superfund by pursuing a program of study composed of seemingly frivolous courses. These problems arose in the early years of the GI Bill and were effectively addressed through changes in the legislation and through administrative procedures, as discussed in the next chapter. As for scams and rip-offs, these are an ever-present threat in contemporary society in both the public and the private sectors. But this is no excuse for not undertaking a program addressing a serious social and economic concern. After all, military production was not stopped when it was revealed that defense contractors were billing the government for $400 toilet seats or their equivalent.

While recognizing the limitation of college study and the need for alternatives, we do insist that workers under the Superfund should have choices, including the option of such study. Unlike most adjustment assistance, which effectively gives most workers little choice but a low-paying, dead end job, this element of significant choice in the Super-fund for Workers is what makes it a tool of empowerment enabling these displaced workers to choose how to spend the balance of their working lives.

Issues of Eligibility

If the Superfund for Workers is to be effective, it will need to come to grips with the problems that were built into so-called "adjustment assistance" programs for displaced workers from the beginning of such government efforts. These problems are examined in the next chapter. At the heart of a solution to such problems would need to be some kind of "pre-certification" so that when workers are actually laid off, they would be able to move directly into the Superfund for Workers program. Such pre-certification could be linked, for example, to legislation that requires at least six months of advance notice for plant closings.

The proposal to provide compensation at the average union wage level in a particular industry and geographical region is intended to provide a slight disincentive to workers with greatest seniority so that the program would not be inundated by persons who simply decided they would like a "change of pace" in their working lives and would like to spend four years studying. At the same time, this compensation level would help to upgrade the status of those at the lower end of pay scales in that industry—frequently minorities or women.

Some criteria would obviously need to be applied to determine whether workers are displaced as a result of environmental regulations or military conversions, but the application of these criteria to individual cases should, wherever possible, be made prior to and not after the workers are laid off. There should also be a six-month grace period for workers not pre-certified to join the Superfund program after being laid off.

The question of defining "displacement" is critical. Some cases are clear-cut and unambiguous—for example, when the government itself closes down a polluting facility such as the nuclear weapons production complexes which are operated largely by private corporations for the Department of Energy. Similarly, extremely polluting industries that have been producing banned or severely restricted products recognized as dangerous to the environment, such as chlorofluorocarbons, would clearly meet the criterion of displacement for workers who lost their jobs in those industries.

More ambiguous would be displacement through derivative impact—for example, workers in companies that were major suppliers to polluting or defense-related industries, or farther down the production-consumption chain, such as those involved in distribution and marketing of these products. Just where to draw the line on who is displaced is yet another of many issues that will need to be debated as the Superfund for Workers is given concrete shape and launched.

Other issues that would need to be addressed in implementing the Superfund for Workers program include specifying some minimum period of employment in industry, and coverage of contract and part-time workers. Likewise, the issue of wage levels would need to be addressed. It is increasingly recognized that the minimum wage, even with the recent adjustments, is totally inadequate for a single-income family in many parts of the United States—and in some areas, even with two incomes. The proposal to set compensation at the average union wage in a particular industry and geographical region would be an effective way of addressing this issue. And, of course, opportunities through the Superfund should, as a matter of principle, be available to displaced workers regardless of race, gender, and seniority.

There would also need to be a ceiling so that the program would not become yet another golden parachute for high-paid executives, who may indeed be "displaced workers" but who typically have all sorts of other resources to fall back on, including generous severance packages and handsome provisions for early retirement. Pitching the Superfund compensation level at the average wage for unionized production workers in a particular industry and geographical region would also do much to contain this problem.

Resolving such issues of eligibility would be a difficult but certainly not impossible task. They arise with almost any significant public policy initiative. Although these dilemmas exist and need to be addressed, they are no excuse for not moving forward with the program. In all probability, there would be some initial experimentation, or a period of trial and error where definitions and administrative procedures would be refined on the basis of actual experience.

Redefining Work

Without a doubt, the most radical challenge which the Superfund for Workers presents is its implied redefinition of work. It is not limited to narrowly focused job training which all too often channels displaced workers into lower-paying, limited-skill, dead-end jobs. Rather it asks us to embrace the proposition of education with income support as a positive alternative to welfare, unemployment, and poverty-level jobs and as a means of making a fundamental career shift to an entirely different but still productive role in society. It asks us to assist displaced workers who want to go to school because that is the best way to nurture and enhance our human "capital" which is increasingly being recognized as our greatest economic asset. And it helps to move these workers out of traditional but disappearing industrial jobs into "post-industrial" occupations.

Now that we are entering this post-industrial era, it seems only logical to recognize that work can take many forms, only one of which involves wage employment. At the turn of the last century, four out of five Americans worked on family farms or in other family-based enterprises where they did not receive wages for their work. Today, going to school to prepare for a new career needs to be recognized as a form of economically socially useful activity for which it should be possible to receive assistance.

The concept for a Superfund for Workers is certainly not new, as indicated elsewhere in this book. The GI Bill of Rights provided financial support of education for those who served our country in military conflicts. Are not victims of plant closings and layoffs the lost battalions in the battle to clean up our environment and move to a less military-dependent economy? Have they not been exposed on the front lines to the impairment of their health by working daily with highly toxic substances, and are they not now entitled to shift to less hazardous pursuits after having done their tour of hazardous duty? At the very least, do we not owe these displaced workers a measure of financial commitment similar to that which we now reserve for toxic waste dumps?

A cleaner environment and a safer world would benefit everyone. One sector of our society should not have to bear the major burden of the costs of the necessary economic restructuring. Not only are many of the jobs being lost by displaced workers in the 1990s dangerous to the workers as well as to the environment, they are also often boring and unfulfilling. Three decades ago Harvey Swados wrote an essay entitled "The Myth of the Happy Worker" in which he observed that "the plain truth is that factory work is degrading."[3] What Swados meant by degrading was the noise, filth, and routine of factory work—conditions which have not fundamentally changed since he wrote that essay.

Given these circumstances, it is not surprising that conditions of work for at least some of the U.S. labor force have begun to move in a "post-industrial" direction. This is certainly true for many professionals and a significant proportion of workers in government and management positions in industry, as well as in the independent or third sector—i.e., those working for consumer, religious, environmental, and other community service or public interest organizations.

For most of us, a "post-industrial job" is clearly preferable.[4] Generally, most workers in polluting industries, blue-collar manufacturing, and white-collar clerical jobs, do not experience post-industrial working conditions. These workers should not be denied the opportunity to prepare themselves for a post-industrial working environment which is being taken as a matter of right by many others in the U.S. labor force.

Financing the Superfund

The question of how the Superfund for Workers would be financed and its likely cost under different conditions is important, but it is not the central issue. There is little doubt that the United States can afford such a program. The savings and loan bailout—which some now calculate may come to as much as $500 billion dollars—or the massive corporate welfare program of the 1980s through the Pentagon budget, totaling some $3 trillion—make it clear that we can "afford" almost anything which has generated the necessary constellation of political power. The question is one of political power, not of whether we can afford it.

In Chapter II, we presented employment levels in the various industrial sectors most likely to be significantly affected by vigorous environmental cleanup, toxic-use reduction and conversion to an economy less dependent on military production. As a rough rule of thumb, assuming an average annual cost per displaced worker participating in the Superfund of $40,000 a year (the average union wage in that industry plus tuition and fringe benefits, including health care), the cost for one million workers would be $40 billion dollars. This is not cheap, of course, but the benefits to society, even measured in dollars and cents (let alone some of the nonmonetary returns described in the next section of this chapter) will be much greater—including the fact that these displaced workers will continue to pay taxes and maintain roughly comparable levels of consumption, helping to maintain or restore overall levels of economic activity.

The avoided costs, both monetary and nonmonetary are also considerable. (Unemployment involves not only loss of income but also of the self-esteem which goes with having a productive place in society, and leads to greatly increased levels of emotional and physical stress, including alcoholism, drug addiction, and child and spouse abuse.) There are also direct savings in social assistance, such as unemployment insurance, food stamps, and other forms of welfare.

The Congressional Budget Office, which is responsible to Congress for critiquing the President's budget proposals each year, provides us with the means for calculating the monetary costs of worker dislocation. According to their calculations, a one percentage point increase in the unemployment rate (a rise from 5.3 percent to 6.3 percent in 1989 would have meant an additional 1.3 million persons unemployed) would result in an immediate increase in expenditures by the U.S. government of $4 billion per year in medicaid, social security, unemployment compensation, food stamps, assistance, and interest payments. These expenditures would increase each year that the unemployment rate remained a point higher, so that by 1995, expenditures would increase by $27 billion a year.

But the costs of increased unemployment go further even on a strictly economic basis. For these workers will no longer be paying taxes. The decrease in individual, corporate, and social insurance taxes from these additional unemployed workers would amount to $28 billion a year immediately and $54 billion a year by 1995. Thus, the total costs to the government of an additional 1.3 million unemployed persons would be $32 billion a year immediately and $81 billion a year after five years.[5]

The main principle on which the Superfund for Workers should be based is the one that has been followed, more or less, in the Superfund for Toxic Wastes—namely, that the polluter should pay. Application of that principle does not, in fact, mean that industry carries the full cost of the program. Most of it will be passed along to their customers in terms of increased prices. And as long as all companies in a particular industry are carrying the same burden (and they are protected from low-cost imports from competitors in other countries which are not providing for their displaced workers in this manner), no company will be at a greater competitive disadvantage after the Superfund for Workers is established than before.

The experience with financing cleanup of toxic wastes is quite complicated and has involved, over the last decade and a half, at least three different legislative enactments—the Resource Conservation and Recovery Act (RCRA) of 1976; the Comprehensive Environmental Response, Compensation, and Liability Act (CERCLA) of 1980; and its amendments of 1986, the Superfund Amendments and Reauthorization Act (SARA). At different times there have been various types of taxes on petroleum and chemical feedstocks, waste-end taxes, and an earmarked environmental tax on corporate alternative minimum taxable income. Numerous other tax arrangements have been proposed, including a tax on generation of hazardous waste, a national sales or value-added tax, and tax credits for safe disposal of hazardous wastes. Another source of revenue has been recovery of actual costs of cleanup from responsible parties.[6] The Superfund for Hazardous Wastes, for example, was meant to be used only where a responsible party for a site could not be found liable for the cleanup. The EPA originally estimated that 50 percent of the total costs of cleanup would come directly from the responsible parties. The actual recovery has been closer to 40 percent. The Superfund itself comes from taxes on crude oil and certain chemicals.[7]

The analogy between the Superfund for Workers and the Superfund for Wastes is, however, limited. The latter is confronted with a complex regulatory/revenue dilemma—i.e., the need to generate sufficient revenues to cover the costs of cleanup while at the same time providing incentives to clean up or dispose of hazardous wastes and disincentives to creating it. The situation with respect to the Superfund for Workers is different. Here the goal is to help individual workers make the transition to new forms of productive activity in society.

Another financing mechanism that has been suggested based on the "polluter pays" principle involves holding companies liable for any layoffs which might occur because they saw a nontoxic transition coming and failed to take responsive action to convert their production processes.[8] This approach relies on identifying an individual company that is also able to pay. As with the CERCLA option discussed above, this ability to recoup damages from or tax the responsible party would be the first choice. A fund to cover workers in other situations where a responsible party either cannot be found or cannot pay would still need to be established based on a tax on the polluting or military industries with government revenues as a last resort.

There should, in fact, be vigorous scrutiny of various alternatives for financing the Superfund for Workers as part of the public debate over its creation. But some general considerations or principles can be set forth even at this stage in the evolution of the basic idea.

In addition to the principle that the polluter pays, financing the Superfund for Workers should strive to use the market to send the right signals to polluting industries. Assuming "forward shifting" of some kind of tax on production from polluting industries, the prices of products from these industries will increase because, at long last, some of the external costs of their polluting character are being incorporated in the prices they charge their customers. In the past, these external costs have been borne by society as a whole, and industry has been able to use the environment as a "free sink." This clearly must change.

In fact, therefore, a Superfund for Workers would use the marketplace to send exactly the right signals if we are really serious about protecting and cleaning up the environment. Polluting products would become more expensive, accelerating the search for less costly and more environmentally benign alternatives.

A similar tactic has been tried with efforts to reduce ozone damaging chlorofluorocarbons. The 1991 budget, for example, contains revenue from a tax on chemicals used by industry which cause such damage. In 1991, estimated revenue is $0.1 billion. From 1991 to 1995, that revenue is expected to total $0.5 billion.[9] Industry has no hesitation in stating, as did DuPont management, that "it will be passed on to the consumer."[10] As the volume of business for polluting industries declines, workers displaced in this process would be provided through the Superfund with the means of preparing themselves for entirely different careers in other areas of the economy that would not place similar burdens on the environment.

But individual displaced workers should not be held hostage to the market, suggesting that appropriations out of general revenues or the creation of a trust fund of some kind will be necessary to protect displaced workers eligible to participate in the Superfund program.[11]

What is critical from the point of view of those workers whose jobs are threatened by the introduction of more stringent environmental standards is that the Superfund be established in advance of the introduction of these standards. The whole history of "adjustment assistance" for workers in the U.S. labor market is one of "too little too late." We have already discussed the critical need for "pre-certification" so that workers, once they see their jobs threatened, can make a smooth transition to whatever form of preparation they elect for their new careers or for early retirement. But clearly "pre-certification" makes no sense unless there is a fund in place which can support them once they do make the transition.

The situation is somewhat different with workers displaced from defense-related jobs. Here, the government, through general tax revenues, surely has some measure of responsibility. But so do the defense contractors themselves, many of which profited handsomely from casual Pentagon contracting procurement procedures, including cost-plus contracts that assured companies a substantial profit no matter how much money they spent (or in may cases, misspent) in fulfilling a military contract.

Both the administration and the Congress have finally recognized that the orgy of tax cutting from the Reagan years is over and there must be adjustments that will "enhance" government revenues. The Superfund for Workers need not be a massive burden on the government budget, particularly if the bulk of support comes from polluting industries and if the offsetting cost of savings and enhanced revenues from having displaced workers in the Superfund are taken into account. This brings us to the heart of the matter in considering the question of financing a Superfund for Workers. That question is primarily political, not economic—a point eloquently made by the savings and loan bailout.

When it became apparent that there was a serious crisis among this segment of our banking system, there was never any serious discussion of whether or not we could "afford" to deal with the crisis, notwithstanding the huge government deficits. It was simply something that had to be done in order to preserve the integrity of that system. Indeed, the initial estimates of cost have been grossly underestimated, and current calculations suggest that the total bill for bailing out the savings and loans will come to as much as $500 billion, and perhaps even more.[12]

Given these kinds of numbers in the savings and loans bailout, $40 billion—or even $80 billion—is clearly within the realm of "affordability." The reality is that we need to create such a program for displaced workers from polluting or defense industries because we cannot afford *not* to clean up our environment or move toward a peace economy. The costs of failing to do so would be far greater. Creating a Superfund for displaced workers is, in fact, a positive way of dealing with the issue of job loss in environmental cleanup or conversion to a less militarized economy.

Threatened job losses become part of the politics of resisting either effort. An industry-sponsored lobby group, calling itself the Clean Air Working Group, ran a series of ads in the *New Republic* and other magazines and newspapers in the Spring of 1990 with an alarmist message. These ads claimed that the version of the clean air legislation just passed by the U.S. Senate "could eliminate up to 750,000 jobs and seriously impact three million others."(The *New Republic* ad is reproduced on page 17.) We have already examined the exaggerated nature of these claims in Chapter II.

Industry obviously intended that these numbers would be taken as a compelling argument against even the relatively mild clean-up measures which have just been signed into law. But in fact, these claims, even if exaggerated, are a persuasive argument for the Superfund for Workers.

The version of the Clean Air Act that was adopted includes a provision of $250 million for unemployment and retraining benefits for workers who lose their jobs because of the new law. But this still reflects an old-style approach to the problem. The kinds of opportunities that would be provided to displaced workers under the Superfund constitute a quantum leap from temporary short-term support and retraining for other insecure industrial jobs to providing the opportunity for a fundamental shift in career as the U.S. economy moves into the post-industrial era.[13]

Ripple Effects of the Superfund Program

Education is one of the most cherished American values. We see education as the key to upward mobility, to improving the quality of life, to overcoming prejudice and inequality, to promoting democracy, and to building a sounder economy.

Giving displaced workers the opportunity to further their education would provide them with a sound foundation for pursuing a number of future careers, rather than locking them into a specific job that may well have disappeared by the time they are qualified to take it, as often happens with narrow "retraining." Such an educational opportunity would help these workers to realize their full potential and enable them to contribute more fully to society as well as to their own families and communities.

The Superfund program would also have a direct and positive impact on an important sector of our economy and a major source of jobs. The higher education sector is one of our most labor intensive. At the University of California at Berkeley, for example, it takes 15,000 workers to service 30,000 students.

New jobs would also come with the construction of new buildings and the production of additional learning materials. By providing decent compensation for displaced workers in a new and challenging work environment—i.e., the university classroom—we will prevent the often hidden but no less real medical and social costs of increased and protracted unemployment. By the same token, we will help to limit the adverse impact of plant closings on the economy and the surrounding community and its businesses.

These facts have not been lost on local and state political leaders around the country who are calling for renewed commitment to education. The higher education sector is already the number one industry in the Boston area with 60 colleges and 350,000 students and is helping Massachusetts ride out its current recession. A former governor of Texas has called for making education the number one industry in that state as a way of offsetting economic problems and limited employment prospects in the oil and agriculture sectors. Even groups of business leaders, such as the Committee on Economic Development, have argued that we urgently need to strengthen educational achievement at all levels in our society if we are to remain competitive in the world economy in the twenty-first century.

As stated earlier, the Superfund for Workers must not be allowed to become a new form of welfare for the privileged—in this case, the university. The central feature of study programs for displaced workers should be some form of "contract learning" often followed by "nontraditional" or older students. The content and objectives of such study programs are tailored to meet the individual student's needs and to take into account his or her life experiences. The programs are designed jointly by the student and his or her mentor on the college or university faculty.

Colleges and universities will thus be pushed into becoming more "consumer-oriented," seeking to serve the needs of displaced workers who come to them through the Superfund. Such individually designed study programs, which reflect the life experiences of the workers, offer at least the hope—if not the guarantee—that the end result will be an educational attainment and qualification relevant to the real needs of society as well as the objectives of the individual worker.

There will be other desirable spinoff effects from the Superfund program. We recognize that not all of those who complete four years of higher education will necessarily be able to find wage employment in the mainstream economy that will enable them to maintain their existing standard of living. Hence the provision for partial income supplements if the Superfund graduates seek work in the community or service sector as volunteers (if they elect early retirement) or at lower wages often found in this sector. There is a critical need for people able and willing to work in this sector, helping their neighbors, whether it is tutoring children who are falling behind in school, assisting the homeless in creating a decent place to live, or serving the elderly who all too often need, more than anything else, human companionship.

The Superfund program, by providing this option for some displaced workers, would give an enormous boost to the human services provided through the "caring occupations." Some displaced workers might even elect to become trained as human service professionals as part of or in addition to their four years of college education. In many communities, there are critical shortages of properly qualified persons, in part because levels of compensation are not as attractive as they should be—for example, nursing has become something of a national crisis.

While voluntary effort will never become an effective substitute for government-funded social services, such efforts would get a shot in the arm from the availability of displaced workers taking early retirement after completing their college and university studies, and thus would become available for voluntary service within their community. The potential of the Superfund for revitalizing the sense of community through volunteer service, the "caring occupations," and local economic development from small businesses or self-employment by Superfund graduates may well turn out to be its most pervasive impact on society as a whole.

The U.S. economy is entering a rocky period of rapid and unpredictable change. There are those who argue that programs like the Superfund for Workers will greatly exacerbate such change by accelerating the de-industrialization of America. But this is occurring anyway—witness the recent announcement by General Motors that it is closing down up to nine plants that employ tens of thousands of workers, as it shrinks itself in the face of unrelenting competition.[14] Ultimately, the Superfund for Workers should help American society cope with the dislocations caused by deindustrialization and help all dislocated workers prepare for new careers in other fields less vulnerable to these pressures.

Others insist that the major problem will be lack of jobs at decent pay for Superfund graduates. We are well aware of this problem, which was extensively discussed in Chapter III. The Superfund for Workers is no panacea for all the social and economic ills confronting America at the turn of the century. But we are convinced that without it, the list of problems at the beginning of this book will be even harder to overcome, and the Superfund, by empowering workers who will otherwise become victims of rapid and turbulent change, will help to build a more sustainable and democratic future in the United States.

NOTES

1. See, for example, Edward Goldsmith, *The Great U-Turn: De-Industrializing Society,* New York: The Bootstrap Press, 1989.
2. "Who Pays for Peace?" *Business Week,* July 7, 1990, pp. 64-67.
3. Harvey Swados, "The Myth of the Happy Worker," which was originally published in *The Nation* and has recently been reissued, along with a collection of short stories on the same theme, in *On the Line,* Champaign-Urbana: University of Illinois Press, 1990, pp. 235-247.
4. The Labor Institute in New York has developed a questionnaire that points out many characteristics of industrial jobs whose absence characterizes many of the "post-industrial" jobs:

> Reporting for work at a specific time each day; supervision of work on a daily basis by a foreman, supervisor, or their equivalent; if late for work, subject to an "absentee control program"; not able to leave work to take care of personal affairs at the worker's discretion; not able to make or receive personal telephone calls at work at the worker's discretion; need permission to go to the bathroom at times other than official breaks; phone calls subject to monitoring by supervisors; required to work a set number of hours per week; subject to "compulsory overtime"; required to work night or swing shifts; subject to a drug testing program; no worker determination of the content and scheduling of his or her load; subject at work to a dress code or regulations concerning beards, hair length, etc.; subject to being fired or suspended for disobeying a direct order from an immediate supervisor; working on a daily basis with toxic substances; not permitted by the employer to refuse to do at the worker's discretion any work which he or she considers hazardous to his or her health; no form of meaningful job security whereby the

> job can be held by the worker until he or she decides
> to leave it; policies that govern the worker's job not
> determined either by the worker concerned or through
> some sort of democratic process involving other
> workers.

A number of books have been published in the last decade which attempt to describe this optimistic scenario of future work. Among them are: James Robertson, *Future Wealth: New Economics for the 21st Century* (New York: The Bootstrap Press, 1990); Charles Handy, *The Future of Work: A Guide to a Changing Society* (New York: Basil Blackwell, 1984); and Alvin Toffler, *The Third Wave* (New York: William Morrow, 1980).

While the majority of new jobs in the U.S. economy clearly do not now share many of these characteristics, the Superfund for Workers should be a means by which an increasing number of jobs would move in this direction.

5. Congressional Budget Office, *The Economic and Budget Outlook: Fiscal Years 1991-1995*, A Report to the Senate and House Committees on the Budget, Part 1, Washington, DC: U.S. Government Printing Office, 1990, p. 55.

6. Douglas W. McNiel and Andrew W. Foshee, "Superfund Financing Alternatives," *Policy Studies Review,* Summer 1988, pp. 751-60. See also U.S. Congress, Office of Technology Assessment, *Coming Clean: Superfund's Problems Can Be Solved* (OTA-ITE-433), Washington, DC: U.S. Government Printing Office, October 1989; Rochelle L. Stanfield, "Stewing Over Superfund," *National Journal,* August 8, 1987, pp. 2030-32.

7. As of September 1989, potentially responsible parties have financed 41 percent of all remedial design starts and 37 percent of all remedial action starts. (U.S. General Accounting Office, *Superfund: A More Vigorous and Better Managed Enforcement Program Is Needed,* Washington, DC: GAO, December 1989, pp. 17-18.)

8. This is a method suggested by Sanford Lewis of the National Toxic Campaign Fund.

9. "Cutting the Deficit: The Final Package," *New York Times,* October 28, 1990.

10. Janice Long, "Tax on CFCs to Raise Half Billion Dollars," *Chemical and Engineering News,* December 4, 1989, p. 6.

11. The creation of a trust fund is no panacea, however. Witness the difficulties that have affected unemployment insurance from time to time, especially in the early 1980s, when there were substantial trust fund inadequacies in a number of states. See Wayne Vroman, "The Aggregate Performance of Unemployment Insurance 1980-1985," in Hansen and Byers, eds., *Unemployment Insurance: The Second Half-Century,* Madison: University of Wisconsin Press, 1990, pp. 19-43.

12. "New Estimate on Savings Bailout Says Cost Could be $500 Billion," *New York Times,* April 7, 1990.

13. "Lawmakers Reach Accord on Clean Air," *New York Times,* October 23, 1990; "Bush Signs Major Revision of Anti-Pollution Law," *New York Times,* November 16, 1990; and Representative Bob Wise, "Clean Air Employment Transition Assistance, Amendment to H.R. 3030, Clean Air Act Amendments of 1990" (unpublished statement).

14. "G.M. Plans to Shut Up to 9 Factories; Loses $1.98 Billion," *New York Times,* November 1, 1990.

VI.

LESSONS LEARNED

Lessons from previous programs, designed to help those whose jobs have been destroyed to prepare themselves for new careers, can help in designing more effective programs for such workers in the future. In this chapter, we identify some of the pitfalls in programs tried in the past and discuss ways in which they might be remedied by the Superfund for Workers.

The GI Bills

Issues debated in passage of the original GI Bill included provision of aid to civilian workers in military industries (veterans did not oppose this, but they did insist on a separate program for nonveterans), the war debt and concern over the cost of the program, and federal control over education (which was resolved by decentralizing administration of the GI Bill). Many agreed that war-industry workers should be included as the transition to a peace-time economy would affect a large number of people, which could result in labor unrest and could be quite costly in terms of high unemployment. Even President Roosevelt told Congress that he hoped similar opportunities for education and unemployment insurance would be extended to workers in the military industry.

However, the GI Bill covered only veterans, and Congress failed to act on the issue of dislocated workers.[1]

The Osborne Committee recommended that training for veterans be restricted to areas in the economy in which there was a need for trained workers. The American Youth Commission in 1944 wanted vocational and apprenticeship training to be stressed in the program for veterans/workers as it would take less time and thus be less costly.[2]

In debate over the original GI Bill, Congress argued that it would be cheaper to provide veterans and workers with assistance than to face an economic depression which might result from so many being unemployed at one time.[3] The U.S. budget deficit today is likely to be a source of conflict in adopting a Superfund for Workers, yet it cannot compare with the deficit this country faced in the years just following World War II. For example, in 1946 the Federal deficit amounted to 7.5 percent of the Gross National Product. Today the deficit is "only" 3.0 percent of the Gross National Product.[4]

Problems with the actual implementation of the original GI Bill included unjustifiable increases in tuition since schools were permitted to set tuition rates and payments were made directly to them without careful government review. In addition, schools with questionable reputations participating in the program were among leading causes of abuse of the program.[5] Another problem involved on-the-job training which often turned out to be a labor subsidy to the employer. Employers were not required to pay veterans enrolled in the program at the same wage as nonveterans. Therefore, they were able to pay veterans at a lower wage, and use the government payments to bring veteran wages up to those of other workers.[6]

Veterans organizations lobbied hard for the passage of the Korean GI Bill, which was successful in correcting many of the problems associated with the original GI Bill. It too faced criticisms, however. In order to correct some of the abuses of tuition increases, periodic lump-sum payments were made directly to veterans to cover tuition and fees. This created a built-in bias in the Korean GI Bill against private schools (which generally had higher tuition rates), and therefore reduced the choice of institutions a veteran could attend. The Korean GI Bill also prohibited government funding for courses considered recreational or impractical for career development, emphasizing education which would lead to "useful" occupations.[7]

There was again opposition to extension of the GI Bill in 1957, 1963, and 1964, mainly due to the cost which, it was argued, would add up to billions of dollars over the years. Long-term, low-interest loans were suggested as one alternative, but this was overridden.[8]

Among recent criticisms of the GI Bill provisions are that they favored college over vocational or technical training, job counseling and employment placement programs are inadequate, and society might benefit more from skilled craftspersons rather than persons with college degrees.[9]

The GI Bill sets important precedents to the Superfund for Workers. These include the emphasis on education and retraining—the concern expressed by the Roosevelt administration for dislocated workers as well as veterans—the importance of on-the-job training and job counseling, the emphasis on education geared toward employment, and the continued commitment to financing and administration of the program in the face of opposition over cost and national debt. Above all else, the GI Bill, by providing meaningful choices to veterans and allowing them to make those choices, became a tool of empowerment. That should be the ultimate impact of the Superfund for Workers.

TAA and JTPA

Aside from the GI Bill, two other major programs dedicated to providing assistance to dislocated workers are the Trade Adjustment Assistance Act and Title III of the Job Training Partnership Act. The Title III program of the Job Training Partnership Act is a weakened version of the Comprehensive Employment and Training Act which it replaced in 1982. Both the TAA and JTPA programs are seriously and fundamentally flawed.

Principal flaws of the Title III program are limited funds ($200 million in 1987), the focus on retraining to the exclusion of education, priority to low-cost job search assistance over training, and the shortness of periods for both training (9 weeks) and income support (26 weeks). Additional problems have arisen as a consequence of its being administered at the state rather than federal level. Many states simply do not have the funding, and may not have much interest in helping to relocate displaced workers to other states. This is a problem with the TAA legislation as well.[10] The Title III program of JTPA also dropped the provision in CETA for subsidized jobs in the public sector.

Shortcomings were built into the Trade Adjustment Assistance Act which resulted in long delays in processing claims, inadequate job search assistance, and the condition that TAA funds must cover all of a worker's training (other public or private funds cannot be used to supplement costs). Yet another flaw is the requirement that workers must be in a training program to receive aid, even though not all workers can benefit from vocational training (older workers, for example), especially when most available jobs are in the low-paying service sector. In addition, the program has been criticized for aiding too small a percentage of its target population due to insufficient funding, and its exclusion of workers who make component parts in supplier industries. For example, a worker who makes shoes would qualify, but not a worker who makes parts for the shoes.[11]

A successful transition program for workers has been characterized as one in which:

- Help is available early, preferably before people are laid off.

- Services are offered in one, conveniently located place (e.g., work site).

- Employers and workers are involved in the planning and administration of the program.

- A full range of services is offered, including counseling, training, and education.[12]

But these conditions are still insufficient in eliminating worker resistance to industrial restructuring which provides the basis for job blackmail. Support of displaced workers must be substantial enough to assure that they and their families will not experience major economic hardships, for example, losing their house because they can no longer meet the mortgage payments. Support must be provided for a long enough period so that they have the option of preparing for an entirely new career of productive work. Finally, an effective program for displaced workers must make possible real choices by the workers involved as they seek to restructure their remaining working lives.

Neither the Trade Act of 1974, nor Title III of the JTPA do all of these things, although they would be more effective if the best elements of each could be combined into one comprehensive adjustment assistance program open to all workers. The GI Bill in its various incarnations comes closer as a model for the Superfund because it provided those being assisted with real choices and longer-term support. The goal in the struggle to create a Superfund for Workers in the 1990s is to move beyond the GI Bill in fashioning a program that will effectively overcome job blackmail and enable the country to press forward aggressively with the industrial restructuring that is essential if we are to achieve real environmental sustainability.

NOTES

1. Theodore R. Mosch, *The GI Bill: A Breakthrough in Educational and Social Policy in the United States,* Hicksville, N.Y.: Exposition Press, 1975, p. 40.
2. Ibid., pp. 31, 34.
3. Ibid., pp. 21-23.
4. Executive Office of the President, Office of Management and Budet, *Budget of the United States Government, 1991,* Washington, DC: U.S. Government Printing Office, 1990.
5. Mosch, op. cit., pp. 45, 49.
6. Sar Levitan and Joyce Zickler, *Swords Into Plowshares: Our GI Bill,* Salt Lake City: Olympus Publishing Company, 1973, pp. 49, 54-55.
7. Ibid., pp. 40, 52-53, 61-62.
8. Mosch, op. cit., pp. 59-60.
9. Levitan and Zickler, op. cit., pp. 58, 61-62.
10. Duane E. Leigh, *Assisting Displaced Workers: Do the States Have a Better Idea?,* Washington, DC: W.E. Upjohn Institute for Employment Research, 1989, pp. 22-29.
11. Edwin Bowers, "A Beacon of Hope Could Be Snuffed Out," *Iron Age,* July 2, 1984, pp. 61-63.
12. Office of Technology Assessment, *Trade Adjustment Assistance: New Ideas for an Old Program,* Washington, DC: U.S. Government Printing Office, June 1987, p. 36.

VII.

MAKING IT HAPPEN: THE POLITICS OF CREATING A SUPERFUND FOR DISPLACED WORKERS

Defining the Superfund Objective

The task of creating the Superfund for Workers must begin with a clear statement of objectives such as the following:

> Workers who lose their jobs as a result of the effort to clean up the environment, reduce toxics, protect workers' or the public's health and safety, or convert to an economy less dependent on military production should not lose substantial income or benefits, but should instead be offered the opportunity to prepare for new careers.

The Superfund for Workers provides that these workers will be given up to four years of assistance at the average union wage and benefits in their industry and geographic region, plus tuition to go to any accredited post-secondary educational institution or engage in a similar program to prepare for a new career.

Coalition-Building

As with any major departure in public policy, it will be necessary to build a broad base of political support for the concept of a Superfund for Workers. The first step in building such a coalition will be to get as many public interest groups as possible to subscribe to the above objective by pledging that they will not support bans or phase-outs in toxic-use reduction legislation unless and until that legislation also includes provisions for establishing a fund to protect workers. The environmental community is an obvious target, but it is now well established that the vast majority of Americans, whether or not they belong to an environmental organization, support the cleanup of our environment. However, coalition-building should not stop there. Consumer, church, women's groups, senior citizens, and other constituencies should be enlisted in the cause, as well as the higher education community which would reap substantial benefits from the influx of fully funded students. Even progressive elements in the business community who understand that we have no alternative but to clean up our environment should be enlisted in this cause.

There is also broad support among Americans today, with the end of the Cold War, to reduce military production and to devote a significant proportion of the vast sums that have been spent on defense for constructive social purposes. Enlarging the Superfund for Workers to encompass those who lose their jobs due to defense spending cutbacks as well as those who lose their jobs through environmental cleanup should broaden substantially the appeal of this initiative.

The usual political "logrolling" that goes on in building a coalition of the broadest possible support for the Superfund for Workers will doubtless occur. Trade unions and other worker groups would be more likely to pledge support for toxic-use reduction bills if those bills contained provisions for a Superfund for Workers.

Working People and the Populist Decade of the 1990s

The meaningful extent and effectiveness of coalition-building on behalf of the Superfund for Workers will be a function of the emergence of working people as a new political force in American society. The stage is set by the public reaction to the excesses of the Reagan years in the 1980s that is beginning to set in. In a recent article based on his newest book, *The Politics of Rich and Poor: Wealth and the American Electorate in the Reagan Aftermath,* Kevin Philips, a conservative political analyst, notes that while in 1980 corporate chief executive officers made roughly 40 times the income of average factory workers, by 1989 they were making 93 times as much. During that same period, the net worth of the *Forbes* 400 richest Americans nearly tripled.[1] As we have demonstrated elsewhere in this book, especially Chapter III, real wages of American workers have been dropping steadily during the 1980s until they are now lower than they were 30 years ago. Likewise inequality of income distribution has increased to the point where it is more unequal than it was in 1950.[2]

History is on the side of those who believe that with the new decade a populist reaction will set in—as Philips notes that it did on two previous occasions in this century after similar periods of greed, glitz, and excessive concentration of wealth. It is certainly time for such a populist reaction because working people really took a beating in the 1980s, not only in terms of income but also political participation and influence as the percentage of American workers belonging to trade unions dropped to a new low—at 16.4 percent this portion is far, far less than that of any other major industrialized country.[3]

Sometimes it takes real adversity to create sufficient motivation for action. The plea of Tony Mazzocchi of the Oil, Chemical and Atomic Workers International Union and others for the labor movement seriously to consider creating an alternative to the existing major parties—both of which have done precious little good and a lot of harm to the interests of working people during the 1980s—comes at a propitious and timely moment.

"The needs and priorities of working people are being ignored in the present political climate," Mazzocchi writes, "and our only hope is to try to change that climate by creating a political entity that can put forward an alternative agenda for the nation." He goes on to observe that while this is a "daunting task," it is not an impossible one:

> The civil rights movement of the 1960s changed the way the
> government dealt with problems of minorities in the U.S.,
> and the women's movements of the 1970s changed the way
> it approached the problems of women. In the same way, the
> labor movement of the 1990s can change the way govern-
> ment deals with the problems of workers, if only laborers
> prepare to take drastic action.[4]

A centerpiece of that political movement should be the Superfund
for Workers. It addresses a central concern of working people as we
enter a new decade bound to be characterized by widespread economic
restructuring. In the 1980s, which also experienced extensive restructuring, working people paid dearly. That should not happen again, and
the Superfund for Workers will help to prevent it.

The Vision of a New America

While the process of coalition-building is a crucial element in creating sufficient political momentum for the Superfund to happen, it is important that this effort be shaped by a broader vision of the American
future. One vital dimension of that vision embraces the proposition that
"human capital" is our most vital national resource and must not only
be sustained but nurtured. The Superfund for Workers is a program
designed for this emerging era. It seeks to promote an environment in
which people willingly share their knowledge, skills, and resources with
one another as they join together in moving into this new era. Robert
Reich of the Harvard Business School calls this new era of "human capital" the "Next American Frontier."[5]

Failure to establish a Superfund for workers displaced by environmental cleanup or military conversion will surely lead to further erosion
of our society. Workers faced with the prospect of losing their livelihood
will fight tooth and nail to protect their jobs, even if it means continued
damage to the environment or bloated military budgets. History reminds
us that this kind of decay of civic virtue usually reflects a more general
decline in social mobility and a consolidation of economic privilege.
These social rigidities, in Reich's view, erode the capacity to adapt and
hence accelerate economic decline.[6]

To paraphrase Reich, we will be able to conquer unemployment,
increasing inequality of income distribution, poverty, and environmental degradation only to the extent that we harness the energy and ideals
of all our citizens in the process of building a socially just, environmen-

tally secure future.[7]

The burdens and benefits must be spread equitably, making good the losses attendant upon the economic change essential to preserve and restore our environment while striving for justice and decency. The notion that social justice must be sacrificed for the sake of environmental well-being or economic prosperity is wrong. Social justice is not a luxury bought at the expense of national economic health and environmental well-being. It is the means for achieving and maintaining that health and well-being. The Superfund for Workers is a vital component of that means.

Yet another part of that vision of the American future is one in which economic democracy will truly flourish. The concentration of wealth and power that has occurred in recent decades, especially the 1980s, is corrupting the democratic values on which this nation was founded. That is why the Superfund is so important as a tool of empowerment for workers who will be able to make real choices about their working lives.

Environmentalists and others who support the Superfund because it offers a way out of the environmental mess we are in must understand that while it does that, its overriding significance is its potential for strengthening economic democracy. The Superfund for Workers is not a soft option for cleaning up the environment—and thus an easy way out of the jobs/environment dilemma. It is a hard option that will be realized only through a long and difficult struggle to create a more just and democratic society for all Americans.

Creating a New National Consensus

Along with the vision of a new America in which we harness the energy and ideals of all our citizens in the process of building a socially just, environmentally secure future, the campaign for the Superfund for Workers will need to hammer away at two other themes. One is the growing and increasingly urgent need for such an initiative as the pressures for restructuring grow and the restructuring itself accelerates. This point has been stressed repeatedly throughout this book and need not be elaborated yet again.

The other critical need is to build a much broader public understanding of the need for a Superfund for Workers by the most elemental standards of fairness. Corporations and their executives have long had their "Superfunds" to protect themselves against these kinds of structural changes. Some of these arrangements are at least widely recognized, even when they are deplored by the general public—for example, golden parachutes that provide executives losing their jobs through corporate restructuring with handsome settlements, often in the millions of dollars.

Others, however, are less well known. For example, business interruption insurance allows a company like Phillips Petroleum to file claims for income lost during the rebuilding of its petrochemical plant in Texas City, Texas.[8] That plant was destroyed by an accident on October 23, 1989 that was caused, according to preliminary investigations, by the company's inadequate maintenance lock-out policy (i.e., the failure to "lock-out" the sections of the system on which work is being done), the use of subcontractors for maintenance work, and an inherently flawed reactor design.[9] The U.S. Occupational Safety and Health Administration has fined the subcontractor $729,600 for 181 willful violations.[10]

Even more egregious is the practice, enshrined in the Federal Insecticide, Fungicide and Rodenticide Act (FIFRA), which provided government compensation for lost sales and for costs of storing a product banned or severely restricted under the act. In the case of one pesticide, Dinoseb, it would cost the U.S. government up to $200 million for lost sales and disposal payments to the company.[11] In the case of another banned product, it cost the U.S. government $45 million for lost sales and $145 million to store the product. Needless to say, the workers who lost their jobs because of the ban got nothing.[12] The Superfund for Workers will seek to correct this inequity.

As a political movement of working Americans gathers momentum, and as the coalitions with environmental and other groups are strengthened, it becomes more and more plausible to envisage the emergence of a broad national consensus behind such an initiative as the Superfund for Workers. Our recent political history is replete with instances of this sort.

After more than a decade of debate, failed compromises, and lobbying by environmentalists and the oil industry, the House of Representatives last November finally voted for a comprehensive oil-spill liability bill by a lopsided vote of 375 to 5. In this instance, it took a precipitating event—the Valdez oil spill in Alaska.[13]

But in other instances, the "precipitating event" is simply the confluence of several reinforcing trends—the populist reaction against the excesses of the 1980s, the emergence of a political movement of working people, the rampant destruction of the environment, the acceleration of the impact of structural changes in the economy on workers, an increasing awareness of the unfair practices in the past and newly formed alliances between labor, environmental and peace groups. All of these can add up to the political momentum necessary to make the Superfund for Workers a reality. When that happens, America will have taken a vital step forward in the ongoing struggle to build a more just and sustainable society.

NOTES

1. Kevin P. Philips, "Reagan's America: A Capital Offense," *New York Times Magazine,* June 17, 1990, especially p. 26.
2. Ward Morehouse and David Dembo, *Joblessness and the Pauperization of Work in America* (Background Paper), New York: Council on International and Public Affairs, November 1988, p. 9.
3. The Labor Institute, *Economic Atlas for American Workers: A Guide to Understanding Our Future,* New York: The Institute, pp. 5, 23.
4. Anthony Mazzocchi, "Working People Must Create Political Alternatives," *OCAW Reporter,* January/February, 1990, p. 6.
5. Robert B. Reich, *The Next American Frontier,* New York: Penguin Books, 1983.
6. Ibid., especially Chapter 12, "Political Choice," pp. 255-82.
7. Ibid., p. 282.
8. Philips was estimated to have collected $750 million in business interruption insurance during the 32-month rebuilding period. (Anthony Mazzocchi, "Jobs and Environment: Are There Choices?" *OCAW Reporter,* May/June 1990, p. 8.)
9. Testimony of Robert E. Wages, Vice President, OCAW International Union to the Environment and Housing Subcommittee of the Committee on Government Operations, U.S. House of Representatives, Washington, DC, November 6, 1989, p. 5.
10. Kirk Victor, "Explosions on the Job," *National Journal,* August 11, 1990, p. 1944.
11. Michael Weisskopf, "Banning a Pesticide, Bailing Out a Business," *Washington Post,* October 5, 1987. Despite efforts to repeal this provision, commercial users of banned products would still be subject to indemnification by the government under the current law. (Jay Feldman, "Pesticides: The Feds Step in, but Toxics Don't

Come Out," *Business and Society Review,* Winter 1989.

12. Anthony Mazzocchi, "Jobs and the Environment," op. cit.

13. National Audubon Society, "Oil Spill Legislation Cruises Through House," *Audubon Activist,* January/February 1990.